How a Promising E
Derailed Into a Minis
and How a God of Lo

BACKon
TRACK

T H E

John
Osborne

S T O R Y

John Osborne with Ken Wade

Pacific Press® Publishing Association
Nampa, Idaho
Oshawa, Ontario, Canada

Edited by B. Russell Holt
Designed by Tim Larson
Cover photo by Jon Thomas

Copyright © 1998 by
Pacific Press® Publishing Association
Printed in the United States of America
All Rights Reserved

ISBN 0-8163-1645-7

98 99 00 01 02 • 5 4 3 2 1

Foreword

When Peter came to Jesus and asked whether seven times would be enough to forgive a brother who continued to trespass against us, Jesus' response indicated that our forgiveness should not be limited by numbers.

Often we are more willing to accept one into fellowship who has never been among us than we are to receive one back who has been on the outside, criticizing us. We have great difficulty accepting and forgiving such a one even seven times.

In the story Jesus told of the one lost sheep, the sheep was lost from the fold of the shepherd and was returned to the fold with great rejoicing. It is my hope that as you read the pages of this book, you will share with the Great Shepherd in His rejoicing over one who was trapped on the barren hills of criticism, but through the working of the Holy Spirit and the prayers of family and friends has found his way back to the fold.

I have known the Osborne family since John was a small boy. As ministerial secretary I was involved in many discussions with John and Dianne during the time he was serving as a conference pastor and during his transition into independent ministry.

Later, as president of the Florida Conference, I was not immune from the attacks John made upon the church. I was pleased and my heart was made glad, however, when I learned of his change of spirit and attitude. I must admit that at first I was a bit skeptical. But my subsequent visits with John, Dianne, and the Prophecy Countdown board have convinced me that there is strong evidence of a genuine conversion experience.

The reader should keep in mind that the story told in these pages is told from the perspective of the writer. Not everyone involved in the incidents recorded may see them from the same perspective, and in some situations some would no doubt see them differently.

I was personally blessed, however, as I read this account of God's leading in the life of one of His children. It reminded me once again that all of us are fully dependent upon the Holy Spirit to bring us into harmony with the will of God.

OBED. O. GRAHAM

Preface

When I first heard it said that John Osborne was turning his ministry around and coming back to the Seventh-day Adventist Church, I spoke my reaction aloud: "Watch out! That guy's a loose cannon!"

I hadn't been personally acquainted with John, but through the years I had heard enough to know that he had been very critical of the church and had reconciled with leadership once before, only to go out again and become even more critical. I was fearful that whatever changes he had made, they might be only temporary or cosmetic.

But a friend who had talked to John told me I shouldn't rush to judgment without first talking to the man himself. When I phoned his home, John was cordial and spent nearly an hour telling me about his experiences, how he had come to realize that he had been on a very wrong path. He shared candidly with me the struggles he had undergone in trying to turn his ship around and confessed that things weren't going too well with his ministry since the change. But he assured me that his resolve, and his faith in God, remained strong.

Having had experience in dealing with a number of independent ministries through the years, I was interested to learn more and resolved to maintain contact with John, hoping that perhaps I could help in some way to assure that he was able to maintain a steady course.

Then, as the idea came about of putting John's experience into book form, I had the opportunity to get really involved in the story of his turnaround. Soon I was visiting with John and Dianne and making contacts with others who were familiar with them and what they had done.

John and I have not told this story merely for the curious, although the details revealed here will do much to satisfy their desires. This is the story of one human being who is precious to God and how God has worked in his life. We hope that those who may be discouraged with their own Christian experience may find some encouragement here. And we hope that by being candid about where John's ministry went astray, we may spare others the necessity of trying the same course. We hope that all who read will receive a blessing and be drawn closer to the wonderful Saviour who understands our frailties, accepts our repentance, and forgives our missteps.

KEN WADE

CHAPTER **1**

The hot Florida sun wedged its way under the wide overhang on the front of the Rolling Hills Seventh-day Adventist Church where I was pacing back and forth, troubling over one of the most serious questions I had ever faced. I realized that my whole future hung in the balance as I pondered how to respond to the things I had just read. I glanced at my watch for what must have been the tenth time. It reassured me that it was indeed nearly 4:00 p.m. on April 3, 1995. I continued beating against my leg the small book with a pink cover that I held in my right hand.

What was taking Dianne so long? It had been nearly twenty minutes since I'd called her and told her I needed her to come pick me up as soon as possible.

Scott DesIslet, our video production director, came down the steps out of the truck we called Caleb—the forty-foot, full-featured video production unit that we used for producing programs to uplink to satellite. He turned and locked the door. Both Caleb and his counterpart, Joshua, were still parked there on that Monday afternoon because we had used them over the weekend to uplink our church services to satellite television so that people in home churches all over the country could join in and hear my sermon live. Joshua was the name we had given to our mobile C-Band satellite uplink. These two trucks, named after the faithful spies who went into Canaan and brought back a faith-filled report to the Israelites, were an important part of our mission to broadcast truth to all the world.

"You OK?" Scott asked when he noticed I was still waiting for a ride. "I could take you home, if you want."

"No, I'll be all right. Dianne will be here any minute, I'm sure," I responded. "Somebody probably stopped her to ask a question as she was leaving."

"Yeah, probably so," Scott said. He paused and looked down the street as though looking would bring Dianne sooner. "You sure you're going to be all right? I mean, if you're not feeling good . . ."

"I'll be fine till she gets here—look, here she comes now," I said. A black Acura had just turned off the highway, and I could see Dianne inside. Scott got into his car as she drove up.

I went around to the passenger side. My wife does most of the driving for our family when our son, Wesley, isn't with us. I tell people I gave up driving years ago because I just don't have the personality for it. I'm a Peter, if you know what I mean—I tend to react the way Jesus' disciple Peter did—quick and without always thinking things through before taking action. That can be downright dangerous behind the wheel!

I put my briefcase in the back seat and sat down beside Dianne with the little book in my hand.

"Are you OK?" Dianne asked, a worried look on her face. "I thought you were going to stay here all afternoon editing."

"Honey, you've got to read this book, and you've got to read it now," was all I said in response.

"OK," she said, sounding puzzled.

"I mean, I know you've probably read it before. It's mostly selections from *Testimonies to Ministers*. But you've got to read it again, right now, in the context of what we're doing *right now*, and what we're planning to do next week."

"Let's go home and read it together," she said, putting the car into gear.

On the fifteen-minute drive home, I paged through the book and read sections to her. "Listen to these words God's servant addressed to a Brother

S.," I said, and read a passage. "Do you see it? Those words are written to me; they're written *about* me! God's last-day messenger was talking about what would happen in the future, and she predicted that men would come in the future and do just exactly what I have been doing—do just exactly what we're planning to do in a big way next week! But listen to what she says about those men!"

I read passage after passage while Dianne drove in silence. By the time the garage door at our house rolled open to let us in, she was deeply troubled.

We went inside without even checking the mail and sat down on the couch in our bedroom. We continued to scan through the little book, stopping occasionally to read a paragraph out loud. With each passing moment it became clearer to us that we had been following a wrong path. That we needed a course correction.

Finally I sank down on my knees beside the couch, laying my head on my arms, and sobbed out a question to God. "What have I done, Lord? Oh my Lord, what have I done?"

We prayed and wept and read together for hours. Over and over we asked the question, "What have we done?" and then we knew we had to face the next question: "What are we going to do now?"

The little book with the pink cover was titled *The Remnant Church*. It was a book I had read before but under different circumstances. In fact, I could recall preaching whole sermons in which I dealt with passages from that book, instructing people on how to respond to its message. The book is a compilation made in 1950 from the writings of Ellen G. White. For years I had rationalized away the powerful truths of this little book when people had shared its message with me. Rationalization was the only way I could deal with a message that ran so contrary to the course I was following. Having reasoned my way around the book, I suppose I had put it out of my mind.

Until this day.

I had gone into Caleb that afternoon, intent on working with my staff to edit a new set of videos that we planned to release soon. While the others got the equipment ready, I sat down on the producer's couch and looked around for something to read. How that little book got placed on the table is a mystery to this day. No one can remember bringing it into the truck. But for some reason it was sitting there, and I picked it up. I recognized it immediately, and I knew what its message was without reading. *Oh, well, I might as well read it anyhow*, I thought. *It's good to bone up every once in a while on the arguments the enemy is using.*

My friends tell me I can be quite arrogant sometimes, and I think that's the way I felt as I began reading. I'd been over this ground before and just needed to refresh my memory, especially in light of what we were planning to do the following week. I could be sure that many people would be quoting *The Remnant Church* to me once we proclaimed that the organized church had become Babylon and issued our official call for all true and faithful Seventh-day Adventists to leave the mainline denomination and to join with us as God's remnant for the last days.

But my arrogant attitude didn't last long. On page 23 I read:

> For years I have borne my testimony to the effect that when any arise claiming to have great light, and yet advocating the tearing down of that which the Lord through his human agents has been building up, they are greatly deceived, and are not working along the lines where Christ is working. Those who assert that the Seventh-day Adventist churches constitute Babylon, or any part of Babylon, might better stay at home.

Four pages later, these words heightened my sense of uneasiness:

> God has a people in which all heaven is interested, and they are the one object on earth dear to the heart of God. Let everyone who reads these words give them thorough consideration, for in the name of Jesus I would press them home upon every soul. When anyone arises, either among us or outside of us, who is burdened with a message which declares that the people of God are numbered with Babylon, and claims that the loud cry is a call to come out of her, you may know that he is not bearing the message of truth. Receive him not, nor bid him Godspeed; for God has not spoken by him, neither has He given a message to him, but he has run before he was sent.

Statement after statement seemed to leap off the page at me, mocking my self-satisfied security, forcing me to reconsider what I believed and what I had been teaching others.

"OK, I think we're ready to start," Scott, the director, said, interrupting my thoughts. "You ready, Pastor John?"

It was as though his words had yanked me back from another world. I had become so engrossed in what I was reading I'd forgotten where I was.

I stared at Scott blankly for a moment and almost launched into a flood of words about what I had just read, but I hesitated. No, this was something that needed more study before I shared it with my staff. "You know, Scott, I'm not feeling all that great today. I won't be able to do any editing. Let's call it a day. I think I'm going to call Dianne and have her come pick me up and take me home."

I'm sure my sudden change of plans took my editing crew by surprise. They're used to seeing me come running in to work on a project, immerse myself in it, and keep working on it late into the evening, hardly stopping even to eat. Sending them home in the middle of the afternoon when there was work to be done— that just wasn't like me. They must have sensed that either I was feeling really sick or that something was bothering me pretty bad.

What they sensed was certainly right. I *was* feeling sick, and something *was* bothering me a lot. I had a reputation the world over as a leader among the independent, "historic" Seventh-day Adventist ministries that are often referred to by conference leadership as "critical ministries." And I was one of the most outspoken critics of the Seventh-day Adventist Church, particularly the General Conference. Many times I had stared into a video camera and addressed the General Conference leadership. "How can you allow these things to go on and not follow the counsel of the Bible and the Spirit of Prophecy?" I would loudly proclaim, shaking my finger at whoever might be watching. Copies of those programs went out to church members all over the world, and thousands of phone calls, letters, and donations flowed in from people who echoed my sentiments. Our ministry, called Prophecy Countdown, operated on a $3 million annual budget, much of it donated by people who had been mistreated or who were alarmed over things going on in their local churches or what they felt to be the lowering of standards—people that perhaps, too, had a seed of bitterness because of the way they had been treated.

"What are we going to do?" Dianne asked late that night. "Oh, what are we going to do?"

Dianne is a very strong woman in many ways. She has been the president of our organization for more than ten years, supervising the work of more than fifty employees and numerous volunteers. She has been instrumental in helping to chart our course through mammoth projects such as starting our own nation-wide satellite television network and launching a global shortwave radio ministry. As we initiated each project, she was at my side, tending to details and doing the organizational work that turned our dreams into reality.

I didn't have an answer. All through the night we prayed and studied and shed tears together. There were so many things to consider. We stood at the head of a ten-million-dollar organization that in just ten years had grown from nothing to the point where we now had 10,000 people who were supporting us. We had been instrumental in leading these people, plus countless thousands of others, into deeper study of the Bible and the Spirit of Prophecy. Many commented that they saw me as a sort of John the Baptist or a Jeremiah—who wasn't afraid to stand up and say what needed to be said and let the chips fall where they may.

At this very moment our followers were perched, as it were, on the edge of a great precipice. Excitement had been building in the ranks for months as I preached sermon series such as "The Mark of the Beast for Seventh-day Adventists" and "The Abomination of Desolation for Seventh-day Adventists." These sermons were not broadcast over our satellite network or radio, but we sold thousands of tapes to Seventh-day Adventists. With each series I had been edging closer and closer to the moment I sensed had to come soon—the time when I would proclaim that the General Conference of Seventh-day Adventists had become part of Babylon and that it was time for God's faithful remnant to come out of the organization and join with us as part of the true, *historic* Seventh-day Adventist Movement. I had convinced myself that this was the message that needed to be proclaimed and that our ministry was part of the original, historic Seventh-day Adventist organization. I was equally sure that God had called me to be the one to proclaim the message and to lead His people out of Babylon and back into God's *original* Seventh-day Adventist organization.

I picked up the book and read it again:

Dear Brother S.:
    I address to you a few lines. I am not in harmony with the posi-

tion that you have taken, for I have been shown by the Lord that just such positions will be taken by those who are in error. Paul has given us warning to this effect: "Now the Spirit speaketh expressly, that in the latter times some shall depart from the faith, giving heed to seducing spirits, and doctrines of devils."

My brother, I learn that you are taking the position that the Seventh-day Adventist Church is Babylon, and that all that would be saved must come out of her. You are not the only man the devil has deceived in this matter. For the last forty years, one man after another has arisen, claiming that the Lord has sent him with the same message; but let me tell you, as I have told them, that this message you are proclaiming is one of the satanic delusions designed to create confusion among the churches (40, 41).

Brother S. is *me!* I had to admit it. From what I read, I understood that more than a hundred years ago, God had warned Ellen White that in the end time, men would arise with the precise message I was preaching.

We had spent the night praying and studying. Now it was beginning to grow light outside. "What are we going to tell our staff?" Dianne asked.

"We have to tell them what we've come to realize," I said.

"What about the camp meeting next week?"

Next week! We planned to drive Caleb and Joshua up to Pennsylvania the following week for a camp meeting. Five other independent ministries were going to join with us there, and we had already agreed and announced that this camp meeting was to be the official calling out—the time when we would announce to the church that we had no choice but to issue a loud cry, calling people to leave the Seventh-day Adventist denomination and join us as Historic Seventh-day Adventists.

We would have to change our agenda. We would have to talk to the other leaders and try to persuade them how wrong we had been. I knew I had no choice. I could never continue down a path that I didn't believe in. Ever since I accepted God's call to public evangelism, truth and following what is right have been the most important things in my life. I couldn't change that now. But how had I gotten myself into such a mess? What had brought us to this terrible point where we had to admit that we had been championing a cause 180 degrees off course from where we now knew the Lord wanted us to be?

Only time would tell whether the others who had joined with us on this course would see the light and be willing to change directions with us.

CHAPTER 2

In my younger years, doing what is right was not always important to me, but the desire to follow the truth was deep within me even though I sometimes ignored it. For some reason the Lord endowed me with qualities that made me a natural leader. So, whether I was going the right way or the wrong way, it's always seemed natural to have others following my lead.

Miss Dorothy Matthews was one of the most beloved teachers in the Seventh-day Adventist grade school in Madison, Tennessee, where I was born. She had a positive influence on the lives of hundreds of children during her long career. She taught my two sisters and my brother, and they all loved her.

She was my third-grade teacher, and I thought she was great. I was having a terrific time in her class. I had lots of friends, and our little group had a lot of fun during class—especially during recess. There were a few kids who didn't join our group, or that we wouldn't let into our group, and I suppose school wasn't as much fun for them—especially when I would single them out for teasing or bullying. But as far as I knew, everything was great in the third-grade room. The pastor and an evangelist had come by one day and asked who wanted to be baptized. I joined my friends in a baptismal class, and we were all baptized at the end of an evangelistic series.

Then one day Miss Matthews called my parents and asked them to meet her at the principal's office. The call caught them by surprise, because all they knew about what was going on in school was what I had told them. "Is anything wrong at school?" Mom asked when she hung up the phone.

"No, nothing at all—it's going great," I reassured her.

"You're doing your assignments?"

"Yes."

"You're getting along with the other kids?"

"Sure."

"Do the others like you? You haven't had any fights, have you?"

"Well . . ."

"Johnny, have you been picking fights?"

"Not really."

"*Johnny*, have you been fighting?"

"I haven't hit anyone."

"Well, I'm thankful for that. I wonder what Miss Matthews wants to talk to us about though," Mom said.

The next day my mother, father, and I sat together in the principal's office listening to Miss Matthews explain the reason for her call. The poor woman was almost in tears. "Johnny's a good boy," she said. "But he's very . . . active—he's a natural leader, and the other kids love to follow him."

"Yes," Mother responded. "We've always known that Johnny has a lot of energy and that other kids just seem naturally attracted to him because he always has lots of ideas of things to do. Is he creating problems in the classroom?"

"Let me put it this way," Miss Matthews said. "In all my years of teaching I've never had a situation quite like this one. I just can't teach Johnny. He's disruptive. It seems to me that there are two different programs running in the third-grade room this year. There's my program, and there's Johnny's program. And they're two very different programs! We can't continue to have it that way."

"I can certainly understand that," Mother said. "We'll have a talk with Johnny and see if things don't improve."

"I don't think that will solve the problem," Miss Matthews said. "I've tried talking, threatening, punishing—everything. But nothing has changed."

16

"Then what do you suggest we do?" Mother asked.

At this point the principal, who had been shuffling papers at his desk, spoke up. "I'm afraid we're going to have to ask you to withdraw Johnny from school."

My father didn't say a word in the principal's office. He was a highly-respected physician in the community, head of the medical program at Madison Sanitarium, and it certainly must have been a blow to him to have his son kicked out of school, but he didn't show any outward signs of anger. He was Dutch-English and a man of few words.

My mother, on the other hand, is Italian—just the opposite. She talked nonstop on the way home, worrying out loud what we were going to do, and wondering why a teacher with such a great reputation couldn't handle her son.

I've often been criticized for things I do and the ways I do them, and I can understand people's impatience with me. I'm not one to blame problems on heredity, but I have to recognize that I am a product of that interesting combination of a strong, silent, often rigid Dutch-English father and a vibrant, active, outspoken Italian mother. From my father I've inherited a strong sense of certainty about the right and wrong ways to do things, and from my mother I've inherited a strong propensity for making my views known.

The combination rubbed Miss Matthews the wrong way. And she certainly wasn't the last one to have a hard time dealing with me. By God's grace I believe I'm becoming a more loving and lovable Christian day by day, but I still have a strong sense of what is right, and it's just not possible for me to be quiet when I'm under conviction.

Within a day or two my parents had decided what to do about my schooling. They hired a tutor, and I spent the rest of that school year studying at home where there were no other children to distract me—and no one for me to lead astray into a second program.

My fourth- and fifth-grade years seemed to go all right. I'm not sure that I behaved any differently, but perhaps the teachers gave up and just adjusted to having a headstrong leader vying with them for control of the classroom. My sixth-grade teacher was Mrs. Warton. She was a good teacher, too, but I was dealing with some heavy things in my family. By this time my father had quit attending church and had adopted a totally rebellious lifestyle. He had begun associating with a whole new set of worldly friends. And as a result, he began treating my mother badly. It made me extremely angry, and I think I took it all out on the teacher and any kids in the room that I took a disliking to. Poor Mrs. Warton had a mild nervous breakdown halfway through the school year, and little Johnny Osborne ended up spending the rest of the year with a tutor again.

Over the years I've often thought back about the way I treated other children at school whom I decided to pick on for whatever reason. I know I made things really miserable for them. I've even gone so far as to seek out some of them and to ask forgiveness for what I put them through. I realize I've always had very strong likes and dislikes and that I've never been able to keep quiet or just leave things or people alone. It's been one of the strong points in my ministry in many ways, but it's also created problems. It sure didn't make my school career go smoothly.

In 1966, I went to Highland Academy in Portland, Tennessee, for my freshman year. Frankly, I don't know how the faculty managed to put up with me. They should have kicked me out. I was flying high—a rich doctor's kid, flaunting all the prestige that money can buy for a kid. I especially remember that there were two students there that year whose parents had just returned from the mission field in Africa. Those poor kids had been in small schools with no one but missionary kids all their lives and then to be suddenly thrown into the dorms in this American academy with a tiger shark like me circling and taking bites whenever I could—I hate to think of how I made them suffer.

Something happened to me over the summer though. A young pastor by the name of Terry McComb, an old friend of the family, came to Highland and heard me sing special music at church. He came up to me after the service, excited, and said, "I know your family is musical, but I had no idea. . . . While you were singing it was like the Lord spoke to my heart and said, 'This is your singing evangelist for the summer series.' "

I said, "What are you talking about?"

"I have a special burden for the country folk of Kentucky and Tennessee," he replied. "My pastor friend, Jerry Gladson, and I want to spend the summer evangelizing these dear people."

Well, to make a long story short, we would go to a park in a small town. I would take out my twelve-string guitar and start singing gospel hymns. Before long, we would have quite a crowd. When pastors Jerry and Terry thought there were enough people, one of them would start preaching. What an exciting summer that was as we saw many precious souls come to the Lord! Little did I realize the seeds of evangelism that the Lord was planting in my heart.

By the summer's end I was reading the Bible and the Spirit of Prophecy and looking forward to an entirely different school year. During my sophomore year, I think I was actually having a positive influence at school for once in my life! And whenever I could, I would invite my friends to come to our house for a weekend. Mom has always been very hospitable and also a very spiritual person, so just inviting the kids to come to our house must have done a lot for the school—letting Mom have her good influence on the ones who came.

That's why I was mystified one weekend, about halfway through the year, when I called home and told Mom I'd cleared it with the boys' dean for me to bring almost all the guys from the dorm home for the weekend. I expected her to just ask how many were coming, head for the supermarket, and bring home a carload of food. We had a huge house, right on Old Hickory Lake. It was worth $120,000 in those days and would be well over a million today, I suppose, so there wasn't any problem finding space for as many kids as I wanted to bring home. Thirty or forty guys could sleep on the living-room floor.

But this particular weekend Mom said she just wasn't feeling up to it—could we put it off a week or two? I didn't understand, but for once in my life, I didn't push either.

Saturday evening, just after sundown, my mom and dad decided to go in our boat to the marina around the cove to get some fishing bait. While they were in the store, they heard a lot of sirens but didn't think a lot about it until they got closer to home and saw smoke rising from their property! They had recently had an underground propane tank filled, and something had started leaking. Apparently, the house filled with propane, and when the gas found a pilot light, a horrific explosion took place.

Never at a loss for words, my mom's response to her burning home, even as the firemen were working, was, "Where are the marshmallows?"

BACK ON TRACK

The fact that I hadn't brought that whole houseful of boys home was one of the early signs of Providence working in my life. Mom never really understood why she turned down the chance to have the boys there, but she has always been a person who walked very closely with her Saviour, and we have always thought that the Lord intervened in some way to prevent a horrible tragedy.

At this time, my father was still in absolute rebellion, and my mother was praying that the Lord would do something to bring him back—"whatever it takes, Lord, to shake him up," she prayed.

The fire shook him good and hard. I think he realized all of a sudden how the Lord had preserved everyone so that no one was hurt in the fire, and he decided to turn over a new leaf. Dad decided to start over, so we moved away from Madison, Tennessee, down to Avon Park, Florida, where my father continued to practice medicine, distanced himself from his worldly friends, and started attending church again.

I guess my life has always gone kind of like a pendulum, back and forth, back and forth, because I remember being kicked out of Forest Lake Academy in Florida in April of my junior year. Once again, I had decided I didn't want to have anything to do with God or the church. My grandfather was living in Los Angeles at that time, and I talked my folks into letting me go out and visit him. Of course, I didn't tell them the real reason why I wanted to go to California.

CHAPTER 3

At age seventeen I packed up my guitar and drums and a few clothes and headed for the Golden State, determined to make it in "the business." Show business, of course.

I'd been singing in public since I was five years old and had had a lot of voice lessons in academy. I knew I had a voice good enough to make it, and more than that, I loved entertaining a crowd. It came naturally to me.

I stayed with my grandfather for a few weeks, but it didn't take me long to find a rock band that needed a drummer. We called ourselves Traffic Jam. We would get together in one of the guys' garage and plunk, wail, and pound until we were sure we had a sound that was ready for the big time. "Let's try Vegas first," one of the guys suggested. "I hear it's pretty easy to get gigs playing lobbies and stuff there."

We loaded everything into an old, beat-up Dodge we bought for $75 and descended on Las Vegas, ready to take the town by storm. We did get to play in a few lobbies but soon had to start busing tables and taking on odd jobs just to be able to eat.

Things weren't going at all as planned, and I began to sense some unwanted interference in my life. I knew where it was coming from. I didn't have enough money to pay for a phone call home, so I called collect. When Mom accepted the charges, I put the question to her directly: "Mom, are you praying for me?"

"Of course I am, son."

I didn't really have to ask. I already knew. In fact, for several days I had had a mental image stuck in my mind of my dear mother down on her knees, pleading for her wayward son out in Las Vegas. The image itself was interfering with my concentration, but that wasn't all that was stopping us from succeeding. I knew her prayers were being answered—that somehow her pleading with God to make something better of her son than a drummer for a no-count band was blocking my success.

"Stop praying for me!" I shouted into the phone.

"I can't do that, son. You know I'll never do that."

"Stop praying for me, Mother!" I shouted again, but I knew it was pointless. She told me again that she would never stop praying for me, and I slammed the receiver down in disgust. I ran out into the parking lot of the casino where I had been working and shook my fist toward the sky and screamed, "Leave me alone!" I suppose I hoped that if I shouted loud enough, God would listen to me instead of my mother.

It was only a couple of weeks later that it became obvious to our group that we weren't going to make it. We were barely subsisting by working as day laborers, and we weren't getting any more gigs. I was utterly destitute and too proud to call and ask my family for help. Finally, I had to sell my drum set just to get enough money to eat.

I've seen this kind of thing over and over again in my life. All I can say is that the Lord has been really, really patient with me, and He has always figured out a way to get my attention when I was going down a wrong path. I can point you to at least half a dozen times when He brought failure into my life, just to shake me loose and make me change course.

Usually I'm pretty hardheaded though. The Lord just about has to take a sledgehammer to my head sometimes to get my attention. I sold my drums to a pawn shop, and the other band members (my friends) robbed me of the money I had gotten. They headed back to Los Angeles and abandoned me in Las Vegas.

My hopes and dreams were all dashed, but my mother didn't say, "I told you so." She just wired me the money to come home and saw to it that I enrolled in Highland Academy for my senior year. It was another "two pro-gram" year. I was asked to leave in April, but they let me return in May to graduate with my class. The principal called my mother one time and told her that I had "tremendous potential" (how many times had I heard that phrase used when I was in trouble!) The principal went on to make a predic-tion. "By the time John is twenty-one, he's either going to be in the state penitentiary or he's going to be a dynamic, powerful man of God."

I lasted one quarter at Southern Missionary College that fall. I had de-cided to major in voice and minor in religion, but for some reason the fac-ulty there was not willing to put up with my propensity for running a second program among the student body, so they asked me to leave.

I think that expulsion made me think a bit more than the times I had been asked to leave grade school and academy. I was older and more mature. At last I could see that maybe I needed to "get with the program" if I was ever going to get an education. So I talked my parents into letting me move out to California again—this time to live with my brother, David, who was the chaplain at La Sierra College. David welcomed me, with the understanding that I had learned my lesson about joining rock bands.

When I first arrived in California, I got a job as an orderly in the emer-gency room at Loma Linda University Medical Center. What a sobering experience! You see all the debris of human violence—stabbings, shootings, beatings. One night a man came in carrying a woman who was cut up really badly. As the doctors were treating her, they asked her who had done this to her. She looked over at the man who had carried her in. And after she was all stitched up, she went home with him.

There was one thing I learned from my experience there in E. R.: I knew for sure I didn't want to follow in my father's footsteps as a physician. I had always looked up to David. He's eleven years older than I, so we never inter-acted much when I was a child, but I admired him, and I suppose I wanted to be like him, so when I enrolled at La Sierra I reversed my major and minor, taking a theology major and music minor.

But that wasn't my whole reason for switching majors. I had sensed the Lord calling me to the ministry at the beginning of my senior year at High-land Academy. During the week of prayer I really felt the Lord speaking to me, and I started to think seriously about being a minister. A lot of people had told me I should be a minister because I had the gift of gab and didn't mind going up front and speaking.

But I was having too much fun in school to keep thinking seriously for long, so I kind of put it out of my mind, although I did start college with a religion minor. At La Sierra, I switched to theology and found I really enjoyed it. I got into having regular morning devotions, and I loved the Bible classes I took. It was at this time that the theology department at La Sierra worked out a plan with the Southern and Southeastern California conferences to give ministerial students some preliminary pastoral training at nearby local churches during the summer, and even during the school year.

I know for a fact that the two pastors under whom I interned were determined by God's providential leading because of the miraculous events that surrounded my being assigned to their districts. During my sophomore year, I was assigned to be the youth pastor of the Hawthorne, California, church under Pastor Jim Wolter. And during my junior year I was assigned as youth pastor of the Huntington Park Church under the direction of a missionary named Ron Spear, who had just returned from Africa. These two pastors enhanced my already deep love for the Spirit of Prophecy, which had been instilled in me by my mother, who mentored me in Bible study and memorization. I am eternally indebted for this.

I was also heavily involved in my music minor. It didn't take long for the voice teacher at La Sierra to realize that all my years of voice lessons during academy had brought me to a level beyond which he couldn't do much for me, so he got me an appointment with Paul King, one of the best voice coaches in southern California. I started going to Paul once a week, but soon I was making the sixty-mile trip to his Hollywood studio every Monday, Wednesday, and Friday in the little Volkswagen bug I had driven out from Florida.

It was a busy, hectic schedule, trying to keep up with all my assignments, plus make that trip three times a week, and practice sessions between. I also started working several hours per week as a salesclerk at Lord's of London, an upscale men's clothing store.

I don't know whether it was my increased spirituality or just that I was too busy for mischief, but somehow I managed to stay enrolled at La Sierra for three years without any threat of expulsion!

By my junior year, the schedule and my focus on voice lessons had chipped away at my devotional life, and I began to question whether I really wanted to be a minister. I was enjoying my work at Lord's of London. I had always had an eye for quality clothing and enjoyed dressing well. It was about that time that H. M. S. Richards, Jr., came to the college for a week of prayer. In one of his messages he focused on the ministry and addressed his remarks especially to the theology majors. He said something that I've been told his father often said as well, and it seemed as though he was looking right at me when he said it.

What he said was that no one should go into the ministry unless they simply *can't* do anything else. He paused after saying that, smiling, and then explained what he meant by it. "I don't mean that only untalented, unimaginative people who can't get another job should be ministers. What I mean is that you must feel so strongly called of God that you know that you simply can *not* do anything else. You must *know* that God has placed you in the ministry, or you will never be an effective worker for Him."

I got an appointment with Elder Richards and talked to him about how one knows if he is called to the ministry. He listened carefully as I told him how I had first sensed the call but was now beginning to question it, and he counseled me that if I had any questions at all, I should not plan on being a minister.

That settled it in my mind. If you understand me even a little bit, you know that once I'm convicted of the right thing to do, I'm there. Or at least I'm putting forth my best effort. I can thank my mother for that, I suppose. She has always been a very forthright, honest, and active person, moving forward with whatever she believed needed to be done.

That's why reading that book *The Remnant Church* created such a crisis in my life. I couldn't ignore it. I couldn't just put it out of my mind and continue on with business as usual. I had to do something about it, even if it meant abandoning all the hopes and dreams I had been living for.

After that conversation with Elder Richards, all the steam went out of me, as far as my theology major was concerned. I finished out the first quarter of my junior year and headed home for Christmas with no plans to return to college.

Maybe the return home was part of God's plan for my life, too, because shortly after my arrival there, He gave me the greatest blessing of my life.

CHAPTER 4

I had been sure of my convictions when I began studying for the ministry. But I suppose at that time I was like the seed that fell among weeds in Jesus' parable of the sower. The cares of this world, the deceitfulness of riches, and the desires for other things began to take precedence in my life over Bible study, and they choked out my spiritual life to the point that I could no longer hear God's call.

But thank God, He doesn't give up on us just because we quit listening for a time! In spite of my wandering away from His call, He still had His hand on me. He still had a plan, and He was about to give me the greatest gift I have ever received from Him apart from the gift of His Son to die for my sins. Here's how that happened.

When I left La Sierra, I headed home to Avon Park, Florida. I had enjoyed my work at Lord's of London a lot, so I started looking for jobs in men's clothing stores, but there was nothing available. The area was still pretty rural, not built up at all, so there were only older, well-established men's clothing stores, with staff who had worked there for many years.

I needed a job, though, so I answered an ad for a teller at the local Avon Park Citrus Bank. When I went in for the interview, the head teller spoke with me briefly and told me she would be in touch. A day or two later I got a call asking me to come to the bank. The head teller saw me come in and asked me to come into the president's office. The president asked me about my family background, what I enjoyed doing, what brought me here, and all those kinds of things. After we had talked for nearly half an hour, he told me he had an idea and that he would get back with me in a couple of days. I thanked him and left without any clue of what sort of idea he might have and wondering why he hadn't hired me.

Two days later the bank president's secretary called and asked me to come in again. I was beginning to wonder about all of this rigamarole just to become a bank teller. When I arrived, I was ushered into the president's office again, and the president introduced me to the chairman of the board. He took me through a lot of the same questions the president had asked on my previous visit. Then they thanked me, saying they would be in touch.

Now I was really puzzled. I couldn't imagine that everyone who wanted to be a teller had to be interviewed by both the president and the board chairman. I felt there must be something wrong and began to despair of ever getting a job at the bank.

But, as promised, I did get another call from the president's secretary asking me to come in a fourth time. This time I met with the president and chairman again.

"John," the chairman said, "I don't think we can hire you as a teller."

Now I was really wondering what in the world was going on. Why all of this just to tell me he couldn't hire me?

"But," he continued, "we'd like to offer you a different job, if you're interested. You see, we just recently created a new position for the two banks that the board controls, and we've been looking for someone who could fill it. After I talked with you on Monday, I knew you were the right man for the job, but I needed to talk it over with the board members before I could offer it to you. They're all in agreement, so we'd like to offer you a position with our banks as the public relations director."

I could hardly believe my ears as he went on to explain that as the PR director for two banks I would be in charge of all advertising and publicity and that I would have a $40,000 budget to work with. No way was I about to turn down an opportunity like that!

I launched into my new job with my usual enthusiasm. The bank sent me to classes on public relations and advertising, and I started attending all kinds of functions as the bank's representative. It was pretty heady stuff for a fellow who hadn't even finished college.

Soon I had come up with a publicity campaign built around the fact that the bank in Avon Park was called the Avon Park *Citrus* Bank. We painted the outside of the building in citrus colors—lime green, orange, and lemon yellow. (I know it sounds pretty gaudy by today's standards, but remember, this was 1974. Earth tones were "in.") We got new uniforms for the tellers, also in citrus colors, and redid the interior of the bank, which was looking pretty tacky. I almost had a teller revolt at one point when they heard about the new uniforms, but after it all came together, everyone was really happy. It was like I had brought the bank from the forties into the seventies almost overnight, and they started having a lot more positive attitude about the place.

At that time, I was attending the Avon Park church and singing in the choir, and one Sabbath morning an angel came to church.

Well, not a literal angel, but I was sitting there in the choir when the most beautiful blonde walked in and sat down next to a man I vaguely knew as Al Smith. All I could see were those beautiful brown eyes looking out from under those golden bangs. I was stricken but also troubled because when she walked in, there was a little blond girl that looked like her who came in with her and sat down beside her. I figured it must be her daughter. I whispered to Jim Crabtree, my brother-in-law, who was sitting next to me, "Who is that girl?"

"That's Al Smith's sister," he replied.

"Oh, but she must be married," I said. "She's got a little girl with her."

"No, no, that's Al's little girl," Jim said.

I didn't hear a word the preacher said that day. I was just trying to figure out how in the world I was going to get to meet this girl. When the service ended, I almost ran to the choir room, pulled my robe off over my head, and shouted to Jim to put the robe away for me. I dashed outside and ran around to the front of the church and took up a position leaning against one of the pillars when she came out.

I was in love! You can say what you want about love at first sight, but I was just smitten. I watched her go down the steps and go to her car—it was a 240-Z, and then I knew for sure I was in love! I knew I had to meet her, but how?

BACK ON TRACK

For three days I couldn't think of anything else, and then I finally realized that it wasn't going to just happen. I had to make it happen.

I'm telling you this so you'll understand a little bit about how I operate in life. I can't just sit back and be a spectator. I have to take the bull by the horns and ride!

By Tuesday evening I had decided I had to do something, and with me the direct approach is always best. I put on jeans, a T-shirt, and sandals and drove over to Al's house and knocked on the door.

Al's wife, Carol, came to the door. "Well hi, Johnny," she said when she saw me.

"Carol," I said, "I understand there's a beautiful woman here, and I want to meet her!"

She started laughing hard, but she invited me in and called Dianne. Well, about five minutes later, out came this beautiful young woman, and we sat and talked for a few minutes. Then I had another idea.

"Would you like to go bowling?" I asked. "My whole family is going bowling tonight, and I just wondered if you'd like to come along."

She told me later that it sounded like fun, but she was a little worried because she figured that with the whole family going bowling together, we must do this pretty regularly, and we must all be pretty good at it. But anyhow, she said Sure, she'd love to go.

I hurried out to my car and made a mad dash for home. As soon as I got there, I ran into the house. Fortunately it was my father's night off, so he and my mother were both there. Jim and my sister Judee were there too. "Hey, everybody," I announced. "Come on, get together. We're all going bowling!" It was the first they had heard of our planned family outing, but they all agreed to play along.

Dianne says she felt a bit better about the whole thing when we got to the bowling alley and all of our family started throwing gutter balls!

We hit it off right from the start. Dianne was on vacation from her job with Xerox in Ft. Lauderdale, and when her two weeks were up she called and asked for a week's extension. By this time she didn't want to go back at all, and you can be sure I didn't want her to go back. We prayed about it and asked for a sign. We asked the Lord that if she was supposed to stay there in Avon Park, she would be able to get a job at the local Adventist hospital. She went and applied and got a job in medical records. Then she called Xerox and told them she wouldn't be coming back. I first saw Dianne on Sabbath, June 22, 1974. Our first date was on June 26. I asked her to marry me on August 10, and we were married October 27. That was twenty-three years ago!

That's what I mean when I say that God has really been kind and merciful to me. Even when I had turned my back on His call to me, He didn't abandon me. I'm not saying that I had to leave college and come back to Florida in order to find the right wife, but I do know that the wife He allowed me to find while I was there has been a tremendous blessing to me and to my service for Him. Sure, we've made some serious mistakes and through misguided zeal have wounded the apple of God's eye. Although we believed it to be the right thing, God has now shown us where we were wrong. We have been willing to stand up and admit that we were wrong, and we have stood together through it all.

CHAPTER 5

I guess you could say that Dianne and I are visionaries. We love having the freedom to develop and run a program. Early on, we recognized the talents and abilities that God had given us and that to utilize them to their full potential we needed to go into business for ourselves. Besides, we loved working together—didn't like going our separate ways each morning—and we didn't want to work for employers for the rest of our lives. Even though I wasn't involved in ministry, I considered that the Lord could give us good guidance about what we should do, so we prayed about it. We asked the Lord what sort of business we should go into, and we decided that it would have to be a business that met three criteria: It had to be something that was needed in Avon Park; it needed to be something we both would enjoy doing; and it had to be something the Lord could bless.

After quite a lot of thought and prayer, we decided that operating a day care center for children met all three criteria. We both love children, and there wasn't any day care facility in Avon Park at the time. We felt sure that the Lord certainly would bless us in providing a service for His little ones.

The only trouble was that there was no place for rent in the whole city that would be appropriate for starting such a business. So we decided we would have to build a place, but of course, that was fraught with its own problems. We were young and just starting out: Where could we get the money to build a day care center?

I went to my parents. They agreed to give us a piece of property they owned right next to the hospital, but that was it. Beyond that, we were on our own.

We sat down and drew up a plan of what we thought the building we wanted would look like. It had room for a day care center in the front and a small two-bedroom apartment for us to live in on the rear. I talked to a local Christian builder and got an estimate, then went to the bank to see if we could get a loan. Even though the people at the bank knew me well, we didn't have the credit history or the collateral they would need, so they turned us down. We were just heartbroken.

We took it to the Lord in prayer, asking Him to give us a sign—to somehow open the door if this was what He wanted us to do.

About this time, the builder who had given us a price for the building was taken ill, and his wife called us and asked us to come see him in the hospital. We went into the room, and we could tell that he and his wife had been crying. "What's happened? Is there anything we can do to help?" we asked.

He looked at me and said, "You know, John, I'm not a very religious man, but I've just had the most profound religious experience of my life. The Lord spoke to me in a dream, and I've just finished relating the dream to my wife."

We were, of course, puzzled as to what this had to do with us. "The Lord spoke to me about your day care center," he continued. "He told me that I'm to build that building for you, and that I'm to finance it for you to help you get started. And that's what I'm going to do."

Dianne and I were thrilled almost beyond belief. We once again sensed God's direct leading—more than that, His direct *intervention* in our lives.

The day care center was a great blessing. It truly was something that Avon Park needed—especially for the workers at the hospital right next door. In fact, it's still in operation. Dianne and I loved living there and being with the kids all day long. It was while we were there that our own little boy was born. We named him after me and after my father, so he was John Wesley Osborne III. At first we called him Ozzie (a common nickname for boys with Osborne for a last name), but then a punk rock artist came along using the name Ozzie Osborne, so we started calling him Johnny. Just in the last couple of years he's decided to go by the name J. Wesley Osborne, which is the name my father went by.

After we had been in business for about two or three years, the hospital administrators decided they would like to operate a day care center for their employees and others; they entered into a lease for the business.

With an established credit record at the bank, we were then able to go into another business that we both enjoyed immensely. We opened a store selling men's and women's fashion clothing in a new shopping center in Avon Park. That little town had never seen such a store, and we made a hit right away. It created quite a ruckus when Johnny Cash and his wife, June Carter Cash, paid us a visit and our tailor made four suits for Johnny. The Cashes were friends of the family. My father had been June's personal physician in Madison, and Johnny had quit smoking with the aid of a Five-Day Plan held at the hospital there. My mother had given June Bible studies. With my background in marketing, you can be sure that I made the most of that celebrity contact!

Within a short time, we had expanded our original store, taking over the store next door to ours, and Dianne added a bridal boutique to her women's section. I added tuxedo rentals to the men's section, and we became a one-stop shopping spot for weddings.

It seemed as if I had boundless energy in those days, energy that could turn whatever I touched into gold. On top of the clothing business, I started selling Amway products and within two months had become very successful and well liked by my "upline." We still lived in the little two-bedroom apartment behind the day care center, but our refrigerator door sported a picture of a beautiful cedar house—our dream house, as they do in Amway. Beside it was a picture of "my" Mercedes 450SL convertible sport coupe. We were traveling to clothing markets on both coasts and planned to go to Europe soon. We were into the business world and Amway in a big way and loving it.

We continued attending church, but thoughts of serving the Lord as a profession were the farthest thing from my mind.

Then Elder Lester Pratt, a conference evangelist, came to town to hold meetings. The team got me to some of the meetings by asking me to sing, and one night Lester really got through to me. His preaching moved me to tears. I went out into the parking lot and stared up at the sky—the same sky I had shaken my fist at in Las Vegas just a few years earlier—and I prayed to God: "If only I could move souls, preparing them for the kingdom of heaven the way that man does!"

When I left La Sierra, I said that if God ever wanted me in the ministry, He'd have to write it in flaming letters in the sky. Well, there were no flaming letters, but I was convicted that at least I needed to make some changes in my life. First was to put away the TV.

Running the store, Dianne and I had gotten in the habit of getting up late—we didn't have to be to the store until almost ten in the morning. We'd work there until nine at night, then come home and eat and turn on the TV and watch it until Johnny Carson signed off at one in the morning.

I loved to watch Johnny—I identified with him somehow—he was a totally uninhibited ham, and I remember thinking *I could do that!*

But now I was convicted that I needed to put the TV away, so I unplugged it and stuck it in a closet. Going one better, I put a copy of *The Great Controversy* in its place. The next night when we got home, I automatically went to turn on the TV, and I must admit to being a bit irritated when I saw the book there instead, but it reminded me of my decision, so I sat down and started reading.

I did that night after night, for weeks. The Lord started working on me, softening up my conscience more and more. I began to see that having a successful business and making a lot of money wasn't the most important thing in the world. But I didn't have any idea what to do about it, except to pray and ask for guidance. "Lord, just give me a handle—help me to know what to do with my life," I pleaded.

It was June of 1979 when I awoke one morning at 4:30 and heard a voice—not an actual audible voice, but it was just as real to me as if someone had walked into the room and spoken to me. "John," it said, "I'm calling you to be a public evangelist."

It wasn't flames in the sky, but it sure got my attention. I lay in bed, just trembling, for nearly two hours. Finally, a little after six, Dianne woke up. "Sweetheart," I said, "You're not going to believe what just happened. The Lord just called me to the ministry."

She was barely awake, but she had an instant response. "I'm glad He called you, because He sure hasn't called me!"

CHAPTER 6

I heard the Lord calling me to be an evangelist in June of 1979, but Dianne couldn't hear the voice at all. Things were going great at our store; we enjoyed working together, and the Lord was blessing us. She could see no reason at all why we should leave all that behind and study for the ministry. She had married a businessman, not a minister, and she couldn't see herself in the role of a pastor's wife. I think she felt that maybe a pastor's wife had to go around with a little bun on top of her head and wearing long, high-neck dresses and black pumps. This was a woman who organized fashion shows. She was a style leader in our town, and the image of a pastor's wife didn't appeal to her in the least.

I began to feel really confused—if the Lord was calling me, why couldn't He let my wife know about the call too?

It's never been easy for me to ignore conviction. Once I get an idea in my head and believe that it's something the Lord wants me to do, I usually act quickly—sometimes rashly, I suppose—without giving due consideration or prayer or seeking the counsel of others to see just *how* the Lord wants me to go about fulfilling His plan.

This isn't just a *spiritual* problem for me; it's a problem in other areas as well. I suppose it was that same spontaneity and jumping from one thing to another without thinking of the consequences that kept the other kids in my schoolroom entertained but drove my teachers to distraction. But I believe the Lord can turn our natural propensities into something good if we will dedicate them to Him.

This time, though, I wasn't free to just jump into anything. I had a wife and son to consider and business commitments and loans that I couldn't just walk away from. I pondered and prayed for weeks but saw no solution. Finally I told the Lord that it was His problem—that if He wanted me to go back to college and finish my ministerial studies, He was going to have to work out a way and make Dianne aware of it.

Toward the end of that summer, I began to realize that the time to decide—to act or not to act—had come. School would be starting soon up at Southern Missionary College (now Southern Adventist University), and if I was going to be enrolled, I needed to at least go up and check things out.

"Sweetheart," I said one morning, "I need to go up to SMC and see about enrolling for the fall quarter."

"Are you out of your mind?" she replied. "Just look at what you're saying. Here we are, in our twenties, and we're in business for ourselves. We have a beautiful clothing store. We'll soon be able to put a down payment on our dream house . . ." she broke off in utter disbelief. I could understand her feelings. We had all the trappings of success—a gorgeous 3,000 square foot clothing store, a ski boat, two cars, including a brand new Jeep Wagoneer, and we were moving forward with our planned lakefront dream home.

"But dear, I think I just need to go up there and check things out—see what the possibilities are. Maybe it won't work out at all, but I'll never feel right if I don't at least go up there and see what the possibilities are."

Dianne sat in an armchair across the tiny living room from me. Our son played quietly in his playpen nearby. She looked at him, looked back at me, and I could see tears welling up in her eyes as she quickly turned to look back at Ozzie. She was torn, I knew. She could see a bright future for us and for our son if we were to stay in Avon Park. The other path, studying for the ministry, moving about from place to place, living from paycheck to paycheck, hoping to make ends meet, seemed dark by comparison.

She watched Ozzie play for what seemed like a long time then finally turned back to me. "We'd have to be really sure it was God's plan," she said.

"Yes, of course. We'll . . . we'll have to be really sure. We'll . . . we'll put out a fleece. We'll put the Lord to the test and see if He shows us it's His will." Surprise and relief flooded over me as the reality of what Dianne had said sank in. It was one of the very few times in my life that I hardly had words to speak.

We prayed together then for the Lord's guidance, and soon we had come up with a set of three conditions that all needed to be fulfilled if we were to close our business and go back to college.

We decided that we would drive up to SMC, and the first condition was that the school had to accept me into the theology program. It had been nine years since they had expelled me, so it didn't seem likely that I would be denied entry, but I wanted them to agree to accept all my credits from La Sierra as well. Our second condition was that Dianne would be able to find work, and third, we needed to be able to find a suitable place to live.

With our conditions in place, we made the seven-hundred-mile drive up to Collegedale, Tennessee, starting out on a Wednesday morning so that we would have Thursday and Friday to check into things. The first condition was fulfilled rather quickly by a visit to the registrar's office. So at least I would be welcome to come, if the other conditions were fulfilled.

We inquired about employment opportunities for Dianne in the area, but nothing looked very promising. So we put that condition on hold for the moment and went looking for places that might be for rent. On a trip to Chattanooga, we noticed a vacant storefront with a "For Lease" sign in the window. That started us thinking about work that Dianne definitely could do in the area, but first we needed to find a place to live.

By early Friday afternoon we had located a very nice three-bedroom, two-bath home that had just come up for rent. Two of our conditions had been fulfilled just that quickly. We called the number on the "For Lease" sign and talked to the owner of the storefront. He agreed to meet us there and let us have a look.

It was ideal for a bridal boutique.

We attended church at SMC on Sabbath and spent the afternoon talking and praying about our future. It could still be bright with promise, we decided. We could sell our business and the new fixtures we had just put into the store, sell off the clothing inventory from the men's and women's apparel stores and the tuxedo shop, and keep just the bridal things for Dianne to open a store in Chattanooga. Sure, I'd be just a student again, for nearly two years, but with the assets we had accumulated, we would be able to live in relative comfort.

What is it about me, I wonder, that the Lord has to pick me up by the scruff of the neck so often and shake me in order to get my attention? Why do I have such a tendency to plan and devise and work everything out in my mind about five steps ahead of the Lord?

I had set up my conditions and my plans, and I was willing to accept God's call to the ministry—as long as it could be a *comfortable* call. As long as it could be on our terms and we wouldn't have to sacrifice too much, we were willing to abandon our heady lifestyle and go to serve the Lord.

We returned to Avon Park flushed with excitement, ready to begin the process of liquidating our assets to provide for our future. We advertised a going-out-of-business sale. Suddenly our store, which had always been bustling with customers, became like a marked minefield. It seemed like no one dared to step inside. Despite deep discounts, my three hundred designer suits from big names like Yves Saint Laurent and Nino Cerruti became like lepers' garments. No one would touch them. The brand new chrome and glass store fixtures didn't attract anyone's interest. We had just put new plush purple carpet throughout the store and figured we could sell it to the next occupants, but they didn't want it.

Even after selling all the inventory we could, we were left with barely enough money to pay off our creditors. I advertised our ski boat for $10,000 and finally had to sell it for $2,500. Oh, how we prayed and wondered—why would the Lord treat us this way? It seemed that as soon as we decided to answer His call, He took His hand of blessing away from us. While we were in business for ourselves, it seemed as if everything we touched turned to gold. Now that we had chosen to serve the Lord, all we had turned to ashes.

I can remember driving out of Avon Park in a U-Haul truck with tears streaming down my face, singing a song my academy voice teacher had taught me: "Though the road may be rough where He leads me, still His footprints I plainly can trace, and the trials of earth will be nothing, when I look in my dear Saviour's face." I remember looking in the mirrors of that truck and seeing Dianne following me in our new car. (Before the idea of returning to college had come about, we had committed ourselves to trading in the Wagoneer on a new Oldsmobile Cutlass.) Ozzie was just old enough to be standing up. He was standing there beside her in the front seat, and I couldn't help wondering what sort of mess I was leading my family into—what in the world the Lord had in store for us in the future, if this was the way our journey into His work was beginning.

CHAPTER 7

We arrived at Southern Missionary College in the fall of 1979, just in time to get caught in the midst of one of the greatest theological debates in Seventh-day Adventism. It was the time when the church was struggling with what to do about the teachings of Dr. Desmond Ford, a professor at Pacific Union College, but the controversy ran deeper than that. Professors in my classes were making statements that I couldn't believe were coming from the mouths of Seventh-day Adventist ministers. It seemed to me that every fundamental doctrine of our church was under attack right in the classroom and that I was the only one willing to speak up in favor of our denomination's historical position on issues such as the prophetic gift of Ellen G. White, character perfection, and the sanctuary doctrine. I'm sure there were others as well, but most of the theology students were eighteen to twenty years old. I was twenty-eight, had a firm foundation in the Spirit of Prophecy, and was not as open to spurious new ideas. Of course, I was quite outspoken about my thoughts as well. I began to feel more and more alone. As I reflect, this experience had a profound impact on my future ministry.

Things weren't much better at home. We began to feel alone and abandoned by God as well. Dianne's bridal boutique didn't do well at all, and our meager savings quickly dwindled down to nothing. One particular Friday afternoon stands out in my memory.

We were flat broke. We didn't have a dollar to our name, very little food in the house, no gas in the car, and the electricity bill was overdue. The power company had given us the last possible extension and had finally notified us that it didn't matter how cold the weather was outside, they were coming out on Friday afternoon to shut off our power because we owed them twenty-nine dollars and we had no source of income. I had tried to get jobs at local factories doing menial labor but had been turned down every time as overqualified!

All we could do was pray. I know now that the Lord was trying to help us to learn to depend more on Him, to know that He is trustworthy. But at that time it was terrible; we just didn't know which way to turn. We literally had lost *everything*—all the capital we had built up in our two businesses, all our savings. Everything was gone, and our faith was waning. We were about to lose it, too, as we considered that we were going to be without heat or power. It was cold outside, and we had a little boy to take care of, and we didn't even have money for groceries.

So we did the only thing we could do. We just knelt down in the house and pled with the Lord, "Lord help us, or we perish!"

Within an hour after that, someone knocked on our front door. I went to the door and found two guys from the college there. One of them said, "Hey, I hear you have some suits for sale here."

"No, I replied, I don't have any left," but then suddenly I remembered. "Well, I guess I do have one left, but it's an odd size—I haven't been able to sell it. It's a 39 short quad." (In case you don't remember those days, a quad was a polyester suit with two pairs of pants and a reversible vest.)

"Well, let me try it on," he replied. "I do take a short."

The suit fit him perfectly. He loved it and paid me fifty dollars for it on the spot. It had originally retailed for over $200, but I was happy. As I watched him count out five ten-dollar bills from his wallet, it was like the biggest sale of my life. I'm sure he didn't know what in the world was going on, but I was so excited I could hardly keep from shouting "Thank You, Lord! Thank You! Thank You! Thank You! Thank You!" with each bill.

What a prayer session—what a thanksgiving session—we had in our little living room after that, weeping and praying and praising the Lord. Little Ozzie must have wondered what in the world was wrong with his parents, but we were just overcome with the sense of God's leading and His provision for us.

Then we hopped in our car and drove down to the power company office and paid our twenty-nine-dollar bill so they wouldn't shut off the electricity. We put ten dollars' worth of gas in the car and bought eleven dollars' worth of food. (You might wonder why we didn't take any tithe out of the money I got for the suit. In reality I sold it for a lot less than it cost me to buy it, so there was no income or profit, but at least we had a little cash to see us through.)

We got home just before sundown that Friday evening, and what a prayer and praise session we had! Our problems weren't over by any means, but we could see that God had not abandoned us. Similar things happened again and again as the Lord led us into a new understanding of the meaning of walking by faith.

I still faced conflict in my classes. I just couldn't agree with a lot of what was being said. But one highlight of our time there at SMC was getting involved in music ministry in the churches around the area. It was as a result of this ministry that I came in contact with Joey and Phil Draper, a young couple who were involved in music ministry for the Kenneth Cox evangelistic team. When they learned of my interest in public evangelism and music, they told me that the team had an opening for a singing evangelist and program director and asked if I might be interested.

They didn't have to ask twice. I had heard the Lord calling me to be a public evangelist, and here was an opportunity to use my musical gift as well as my theological education. Elder Cox's headquarters was there in Collegedale, so as soon as he came into town, Phil arranged for me to meet him.

Phil and Joey went with Dianne and me to the interview, and after Elder Cox asked me some questions, he asked to hear me sing. Phil is a fabulous keyboard artist, and he accompanied me on the piano. Elder Cox also interviewed Dianne and recognized that she has good organizational skills, so he invited us to join his team. I would be his singing evangelist, and Dianne would work with coordinating the campaign schedules.

When I explained to him that I still had another year to go to finish up my theological degree, he said that was fine, but he had thought I might like to study under him for a time.

It didn't take me a tenth of a second to make the decision. To have the opportunity to work with one of the greatest evangelists in the church, and to learn from him—as opposed to what I was going through at college. "Oh no, I can always come back and finish my classwork," I said. "I would love to come and work with you!"

That was how I came to find myself, a few weeks later, in January of 1980, in Panama City, Panama, standing in front of a crowd of more than five thousand people in the Atalapa Convention Center, doing introductions and getting things ready for Elder Cox to make his presentation. I had never been afraid to go out in front of a crowd. I started singing in church when I was five, and I can remember being at MV meetings in church in Madison when someone would dare me to go up front and say a text when they were having some sort of memorization competition. I was totally comfortable and fearless as far as that kind of thing was concerned.

But now here I was in front of a much larger crowd than I had ever spoken to before. I felt a few butterflies in my stomach, but I just started talking with the audience, and I sang and did introductions, and the Lord blessed, and everything went beautifully. At the end of that series we baptized 1,200 people. They brought in four or five portable swimming pools and set them up. It took thirty pastors two hours to baptize all those people, but man, I was flying high to think that I had had a part in winning all these souls for the Lord. I knew now that I would never doubt that the voice that spoke to me at 4:30 in the morning, calling me to be a public evangelist, was from the Lord. My ministry was launched, and I was on fire for evangelism.

From there we went to San Jose, Costa Rica, where the conference had built a huge metal building especially for this campaign. After the campaign it became a church. The place would seat 3,000, but there must have been more people packed in there—standing room only, and people had climbed up onto the metal girders, two tiers high, to try to get a better view. At the end of that campaign, we baptized 900.

I stayed with the Cox team for eight months and then received a call to come to Florida and pastor the Arcadia church in the southwest part of the state. I accepted the call to pastoral ministry, but I knew that my emphasis in ministry would continue to be evangelism. So I purchased a set of slides from Elder Cox and within three months of my arrival in Arcadia launched an evangelistic campaign, using the materials, ideas, and training I had gotten from Elder Cox.

One of the pastors before me at Arcadia was Walter Rea, who within a couple of years wrote the book *The White Lie* in which he accused Ellen White of plagiarism. I didn't pay much attention to that scandal at that time, but one thing I did hear circulating around the conference could have been a warning to me, for my own future, if I had realized that I was just as vulnerable to Satan's attacks as anyone else. But I was flying high. I was serving the Lord, and the thought never occurred to me that I would ever do anything to wound God's church as Walter Rea did.

What I heard said in the conference was that Elder Rea had been a leader there and that he had even been considered for high office in the conference. He was passed over, though, and became bitter toward the conference administration. It was reported that after his book came out, he went so far as to say that if he had only been elected instead of passed over, he never would have written the book!

The seed of bitterness has done so much harm, so often. When we become angry at the way someone treats us or at some slight, real or imagined, the seed of bitterness creeps in and starts to grow and flourish. It chokes out our relationship with God, and finally it can take over our whole life, and we don't consider what it is doing to us because we are self-deceived.

I know. It happened to me later. But as I began my pastoral ministry, such thoughts were far from my mind. I was so enthusiastic for the Lord's work, for evangelism, I couldn't think of anything else.

We moved to Florida in August of 1980, and by January of 1981 I was holding my first campaign in the local National Guard armory, using Elder Cox's slides and sermons. We had twenty-six baptisms at the end of the series, and you would have thought I had baptized two thousand the way the conference president reacted! I heard later that he went around the conference bragging up what I had done, saying I had baptized more people in six months than many pastors had baptized in twenty years.

I felt good about what I had done, but it didn't win me any friends among the other pastors—and I can't blame them for thinking of me as some sort of upstart whippersnapper, considering how the president touted me as his flaming evangelist.

I didn't find out about this until camp meeting the next spring when one pastor came up to me and said he needed to apologize to me. "For what?" I asked. I didn't even know the man.

"For hating you," he replied!

"Hating me for what?" I asked.

"The minute I laid eyes on you, I decided I hated you," he confessed. "But since we've been working together here, the Lord has convicted me that was wrong—you really are genuine, and I need to apologize."

I was completely dumbfounded, but since then I've come to realize that his reaction to me is not uncommon. I tend to arouse strong feelings in people one way or another—either they love me or they hate me, but my personality doesn't make it easy for people to remain neutral or just ignore me.

CHAPTER

W e enjoyed nearly three years of pastoral and evangelistic ministry in Arcadia; then the conference asked us to move to Naples, where I pastored the Naples and Bonita Springs churches. I continued my evangelistic emphasis there, and the conference president told me that if I kept up the good work, someday soon they would probably have a position for me as a conference evangelist. If things went according to plan, I would be ordained at camp meeting in 1985.

As I continued to see the Lord blessing in my evangelistic efforts, I began to come under tremendous conviction that He wanted me to expand this ministry to reach more people. Soon my conviction began to focus on television as the natural medium for spreading the gospel, but I didn't know how I could get involved in something like that.

When I came to the Naples/Bonita Springs district, the head elder of the Bonita Springs Church was a retired Seventh-day Adventist evangelist who had been in the ministry for sixty years. At the time of my arrival in my new district, he was in Hawaii helping in a church-building project. I had never met him before, and upon his return I went to his home to meet him and his wife. I began talking about my conviction to put my evangelistic series on television. A most amazed look came across the faces of this man and his wife. With enthusiasm and excitement, he relayed that while he was in Hawaii the Lord had impressed him that he was to come back to Bonita Springs and get involved in television. He wasn't clear what in the world this impression might mean, but it began to unfold as we talked.

Over the early years of my ministry, Elder Harold Veach's years of evangelistic experience, his personal efforts, and benevolence proved to be a wonderful blessing to me. It became very evident why the Lord had directed Elder Veach to come back to Bonita Springs and become involved in television evangelism.

Finally one Monday morning in September 1983, as I was praying, the conviction became so strong that I knew I couldn't ignore it any longer. I decided to call the conference office and talk to the communication director, Pat Batto. "Brother Batto," I said. "I don't know how to say this—it seems really odd, I realize—but I believe that the Lord is calling me to do evangelism on television."

There was a long pause. I didn't know whether he was covering the receiver and laughing or what, but finally he spoke. "Well, John, if anybody can do it, you can."

My heart almost jumped out of my chest. He hadn't thought the idea stupid; in fact he seemed to think that maybe my conviction was from the Lord. "I'll tell you what," he continued. "I can't come tomorrow, but I have some time available on Wednesday. I'll come down there, and we can go together to visit some of the local television stations in Naples and Fort Meyers to see if they have any slots available."

I was on cloud nine for two days! But our visits to the local stations brought me back to earth. I felt like I had crashed and burned. We were turned down cold at every station. Most had a mile-long waiting list of national TV preachers who wanted to put their programs on the air. I began to wonder how the Lord was going to make this work.

"There is one more possibility," Pat suggested. "Let's check with the local cable provider."

It seemed like a reasonable idea, so off we went to the offices of Palmer Cablevision in Naples. We met with the program manager, but he looked grim. "No, I don't believe we can fit any more religious programming into our schedule," he said.

I wilted like yesterday's lettuce, but Pat wasn't so easily put off. He knew something about the communication laws and cable arrangements, so he pressed forward with another question.

"How many hours of local-origination programming does your cable franchise require you to provide?" he asked.

"Six hours, I believe," the manager said.

"And how many hours are you currently providing?" Pat asked.

"Three and a half hours."

Pat sat back in his chair, looking puzzled, and didn't say anything for a moment. I could see the color draining out of the program manager's face as he waited for Pat to say something. Finally Pat spoke again. "That's strange," he said. "You have a contract that requires you to provide six hours of local-origination programming, but you're only providing barely half of that." He paused for a moment then continued. "And here is a *local* pastor who is willing to provide another half hour of *local* programming for you, but you say you can't put him into the schedule." He paused again for effect, and I watched the manager begin to squirm. "I don't want to make any accusations, you understand," Pat continued. "But that almost seems like some sort of discrimination."

The program manager excused himself, saying he thought he needed to speak with the station owner. I was sitting on pins and needles, hardly breathing, as we waited for the manager to reappear. In about twenty minutes he came back. "The owner is out of the office," he explained. "But I'll be talking to him. Why don't you give me your number, and I'll get back with you."

We left, still feeling uncertain but with at least a ray of hope. The next morning Pat called me with a question. "Do you want to be on at 6:30 Wednesday evening or 7:30 Friday evening?" he asked. The manager had called him and told him I could have one of those slots and that it would cost $300 per week for production and broadcast time.

When I presented this opportunity to the Naples church, they jumped at the chance and quickly agreed to raise $1,200 a month to sponsor the program. I opted for the 7:30 Friday slot, of course, because I knew more of my members would be at home then, and I could count on them to watch. This was in September, and the program was to begin the first Friday in November, giving me just over a month to prepare. That didn't bother me, because

BACK ON TRACK

I already knew what I was going to do. I would use the Kenneth Cox materials and present the whole evangelistic series on television.

When the time came to tape the first broadcast, I went to the station. A young woman met me and told me she would be my director. She seemed remarkably uninterested in the project but asked me how I wanted to proceed. When I explained that I had slides and that I wanted to be able to use them and to point to certain points on the slides, she suggested that we use the weatherman's setup. I took my slide projectors with me, and we projected the slides onto a screen. One camera focused on the screen while the other focused on me. I stood in front of a green wall, just like the weatherman. The station was able to put my slides up behind me, and I had a monitor to watch so I could see where I was and what I was pointing to.

After everything was all set up, I launched into my presentation on "Our Day in the Light of Bible Prophecy." I used the slides and sermons just like I did in regular evangelism and called the program "Prophecy Countdown," which was a title I had seen on a column in the back of *Signs of the Times* magazine.

Dianne had come with me, and she stayed back in the control room watching. She said it was dead silent in there as they watched, and then someone went out and started calling other people to come and watch. By the time I wound up my presentation, right at the half-hour mark, the control room was full of people. The director came out to me, beaming. "You have done this before, haven't you," she said.

"No, I have never been in front of a television camera before," I said. I knew that she was really impressed. It was nothing I could take any credit for, but the Lord had just given me the gift to be able to do that type of thing.

The director went on to tell me about how worried she had been about this program. People in the office had been teasing her all week because she had drawn this assignment. She figured some old country hick preacher was going to come in and stumble and stutter around and they would have to do a dozen retakes. She was so pleased with how well things had gone.

The show literally took off like a rocket. Dianne made a free-gift offer at the end of each program. We had four telephone lines installed in our garage, and we started getting dozens of calls after every show. But the best call came from WBBH, the NBC affiliate in Fort Meyers. Pat Batto and I had visited that station and had been turned down cold. But after the program was on that first week on cable, the program manager from WBBH called and said he had seen the program. "How would you like to be on our station?" he asked.

"Are you kidding?" I asked. "I thought you said you had a waiting list as long as your arm of television evangelists trying to get on."

"Yeah, that's true," he said. "But I saw your program, and I decided you should be the one to be on. Another evangelist is retiring, and I'd like to offer you his slot at nine o'clock on Sunday morning."

"How much will it cost?" I asked.

"Three hundred dollars."

The next Sabbath I presented that opportunity to my Bonita Springs church. The Naples church was sponsoring the cable program for that amount, and the Bonita Springs members weren't about to be upstaged. They quickly agreed to raise the money for the program to go on WBBH.

Soon the little office in our garage became inadequate, and the Bonita Springs church agreed to surrender their fellowship hall to serve as our office. We put cubicles in and fifteen phones to take calls. It just electrified the church. The members were so excited about the program and the chance to do evangelism in this way, and believe me, they were seeing results. New members were coming in all the time.

I could see plainly that the Lord was blessing—that He had given me special gifts for television evangelism—and I began to look for ways to expand this ministry even further. This was the time when cable television was just starting to explode. New cable networks were starting up almost on a weekly basis and linking via satellite to cable systems around the country. We made copies of several of the programs and began submitting them as samples to cable networks. Within six months of going on the air, the Tempo network, with service to ten million homes, offered us a slot. (Tempo was later purchased by NBC and became the CNBC network.)

We were overwhelmed, totally overwhelmed. We had been flying by the seat of our pants for six months, trying to keep up with the opportunities the local broadcast brought. We knew there was no way in the world we could handle the cable opportunity on our own. It was time to look for help, and naturally we decided to approach the Florida Conference to see what kind of assistance it could give us. Dianne and I made an appointment to see the conference president, Elder Henry Carruba. We could hardly contain our excitement as we made the four-hour drive to the conference office in Orlando. We could hardly wait to see the reaction of the brethren when they learned of this fantastic new opportunity.

But what a surprise we were in for!

CHAPTER 9

We arrived at the conference office around 10:00 a.m. for our appointment with Elder Carruba. This was sometime in July of 1984, I believe. Elder Carruba welcomed us into his office and asked us to wait a moment while he invited the conference treasurer and secretary to join us. This surprised us, because we had requested an appointment only with the president. We were soon to learn, though, that the meeting was not going to run according to our agenda.

When everyone was present, I asked if I could have prayer with them before I shared some great news. We all knelt, and in the prayer I thanked the Lord for the way He had blessed in my ministry and the way He was leading to see His word spread to all the world and asked for His blessing in this meeting.

We raised our heads and opened our eyes, and true to form, I launched directly into what I wanted to tell them. "Elder Carruba," I said, "We came here today to share the most wonderful news with you." Excitement quivered in my voice as I continued. "You know about our television program, Prophecy Countdown, there in Naples and Fort Meyers, and how the Lord is richly blessing us. Well, would you believe that we have the opportunity now to expand that ministry even further?"

I paused, looking around at the assembled officers, expecting to see signs of enthusiasm or excitement, but no one was showing much emotion at all. In fact, all three men seemed withdrawn, not reacting to what I was saying, like they were just waiting for me to finish.

I pressed on, excitement raising the pitch of my voice a bit. "This is so exciting to me, because I can see how the Lord is leading. It's just amazing to me. We've been on local television for just over half a year, and now the Lord has opened the doors so that we have the opportunity to go on a nationwide cable *network*. This is so much bigger than anything we could ever have imagined or even prayed for. This is the Tempo network. They go into ten million homes all over this country! And we have a golden opportunity—an ideal time slot at nine o'clock on Sunday mornings! Isn't that just amazing?" I concluded.

Elder Carruba glanced at the other men, then cleared his throat. "John," he said. "We didn't hire a television evangelist. We hired a local pastor."

"I realize that," I responded. "But can't you see how the Lord is opening the doors? He called me to be a public evangelist, and He is opening the way for me to carry the three angels' message to millions across America! It's nothing I've done. It's not me. It's what He has called me to and gifted me for."

"We can see that the Lord has blessed in what you're doing, but you have to realize that you are a conference employee and that this is not the assignment we have given you."

I was starting to feel shocked and a bit frightened by this unexpected response, but I don't give up easily. I don't just roll over and play dead when someone offers an objection. "Elder Carruba, I didn't come here to ask your permission to go ahead with this," I said, my face flushing, my back stiffening. "I only came to share the great news and to ask your blessing upon this expansion of our ministry."

"How much will it cost to go on this cable network?" the treasurer interjected.

"Five hundred thousand dollars a year," I answered.

The poor man almost fainted dead on the floor. "Where do you think we can get that kind of money?" he asked incredulously.

"I'm not asking for any financial support for the program," I responded.

"The money will come. The donations have been flowing in. I'm not at all worried about raising the money."

The treasurer looked at the president, and they both looked at the secretary. Finally Elder Carruba spoke up. "Let me just clarify this a little bit, John," he said. "It's not a matter of whether we have to support the ministry financially or not. It's a matter of who you work for—and not just a matter of authority, of who calls the shots. What it comes down to is that if you, as our employee, sign a contract for half a million dollars to go on a cable network, we then become responsible. And we're not willing to take that kind of responsibility. We have no jurisdiction to deal with a national ministry. This would have to go through the North American Division office or maybe even the General Conference. The church already has *It Is Written* as its nationwide television outreach, so I don't see any chance in the world that we can get approval for this."

I was perspiring heavily now, confused, and totally taken aback. The reaction I was getting was exactly the opposite of what I had anticipated, and I didn't know how to react. "Are you forbidding me to go on the cable network then?" I finally asked.

"John, it's not just that," Elder Carruba said. "We want you to understand that we are very supportive of your pastoral ministry and of your evangelistic efforts. You know we've allowed you to go around to other districts and hold campaigns, because we believe the Lord has gifted you as an evangelist. We're very thankful for the work you've done. We want you to understand that.

"But John, you've got to remember that you are a Seventh-day Adventist pastor employed by the Florida Conference of Seventh-day Adventists. We have an organized work here, and everyone has his own part to play in that work. Our work here at the office is to coordinate this work throughout the state and to make sure that everyone has equal opportunities and help from the conference as a whole in doing his work. You understand that, don't you?"

"Yes, of course I understand that," I replied. "You know I've worked here for four years, and I've always been very loyal and supportive of the conference program. And I'm not asking for any special support or consideration from the office. Just for your blessing in this new outreach. That's all. No finances, no extra work, just your blessing."

"John, we can't give you our blessing. In fact we can't allow you to do it."

I was totally blown out of the water. Totally shocked. Speechless. I just sat back in my chair and looked over at Dianne. Her face was becoming red, and I was afraid if I kept looking at her we would both burst into tears. So I quickly looked away and stared down at the carpet, trying to collect my thoughts.

"But that's not all, John," Elder Carruba continued. "We're going to have to ask you to go off television altogether. It's just not what we called you to do. We called you to be a local pastor."

I was quiet and subdued now, too shocked to even try arguing or fighting. "You're asking me to close down my entire television ministry?" I asked.

"Yes."

"But *why?* You should see how it has electrified the local churches. You should see all the new people who are coming. Do you know how many requests for free material we're getting every week? The phone bank lights up like a Christmas tree at the end of every broadcast. And you want me to stop all this?" I raised my head and gazed straight into Elder Carruba's eyes. "Why?"

Elder Carruba looked away, looked at the other officers, then back at me. He pursed his lips, almost started to speak, but hesitated, seeming to change his mind about what to say. When he finally spoke, it was with reluctance. "I didn't want to have to tell you this, John, but some of the other pastors in the area have been complaining about your broadcasts."

"Hallelujah!" I responded. "Of course the Baptists and Lutherans are complaining. Their members are hearing the truth preached for the first time, and it's scaring them to death."

"It's not the Baptists and Lutherans that are complaining," he said. "It's . . . well, we've had a delegation of Adventist pastors from the districts around you, and they're complaining. Their members are watching you on television, and then they come and attend your church on Sabbath. The pastors are accusing you of sheep stealing, I guess you could say."

"The Adventist pastors are complaining that the three angels' messages are being proclaimed, just because a few of their members are coming over to my churches? I can't believe it. What do they want me to do—put a Pinkerton guard at the door to check the membership of everyone who comes to my church?"

"No, of course not, John. And that's why you have to go off the air. We can't have your broadcasts beaming into other pastors' districts."

I literally could not believe what I was hearing. I had accepted the Lord's call to be a public evangelist, fully confident that all my ministering brethren were just as earnest about spreading the last-day message of the Seventh-day Adventist Church to all the world. Now I was hearing that my fellow pastors were more concerned with their own attendance levels than with evangelism. It seemed like politics was interfering with the real mission of the church. I had never encountered anything like this before and couldn't believe that the conference administration could approve of such a thing.

I tried to explain all of this to the three men in the office, but I got nowhere. Their minds were clearly made up. They had a message for me, and all I could do was respond. "What are my options?" I asked at last. "I just don't see how I can turn down this opportunity. I believe it is the Lord's will, and I'll never feel comfortable in His work if I'm not doing what He has called me to do."

"You don't have any options, John, if you want to stay in conference employment," the treasurer said. "You have to go off the air."

"Let's not be hasty here," Elder Carruba urged. "John, why don't you take some time to think about it? It's three weeks until the next workers' meeting. You think and pray about this until then and give us an answer."

"So I have only two options: Stay in conference employment and go off the air, or stay on the air and leave conference employment. Is that what you're telling me?"

"Those are the only options you have," the treasurer said.

Elder Carruba said a prayer before we left, but I didn't hear much of it. My thoughts were racing too fast.

CHAPTER 10

Our television ministry had been going so well. Funds had been coming in from viewers to help support it. The church members were thrilled. I had felt the Lord leading me into this type of ministry, and He clearly had gifted me with the ability to carry it out. People were telling us that the program was too good to be on just in southwest Florida, that we needed to get it out to a wider audience. That's why we had sent out demo tapes to various cable networks and why Tempo had accepted us in that prime Sunday morning slot.

We had gone up to the conference office that morning with such enthusiasm. Now I felt like someone had kicked me in the stomach. All the wind was taken out of my sails. We were in a total state of confusion, not knowing which way to turn. We had to make a decision within three weeks—would we continue on the conference payroll, or would we follow what we believed was God's call to us to do television evangelism?

Those three weeks were the worst weeks of my life up to that point. Dianne and I prayed, fasted, talked, and wept as we realized the decision we would have to make. There was no happy medium. We had to abandon one of the ministries that we felt called of the Lord to perform.

BACK ON TRACK

How ironic, I thought. *Ten years ago, I didn't sense the call of the Lord at all, and I left college to work in the secular world. Now I have not one but two calls, both of which I believe are from the Lord, and I have to choose between them.*

As we thought and prayed our way through the issues involved, we began to lean more and more toward taking the opportunity that had opened up to us in television. I just didn't see how I could walk away from it. But I still remember the morning that Dianne sat across from me at the breakfast table, and those big brown eyes that had gotten my attention back in Avon Park looked at me with a question. "John," she said. "How can we do it? We really need that check that comes from the conference every month. How can we get along without it?"

It wasn't easy to visualize a future of working for the Lord without any guaranteed income—so many things could go wrong. We could end up out on the street with nothing. We had a little boy who would be starting school soon, and we wanted to be able to afford a Christian education for him.

But I guess you could call me a visionary. While a lot of people sit on their hands looking at obstacles and deciding not to do anything, I guess my sights are just naturally set a bit higher. I tend to look over the obstacles and focus on the goal. I tend to just launch out, believing that where there's a will there's a way.

Hindsight sometimes corrects me, showing me that what I thought was a Spirit-inspired urgency to move ahead was actually presumption or rash flying by the seat of the pants. Pride and anger have also crept in at times and caused me to make bad decisions.

As I look back on the decision we made regarding staying with the television ministry, I wonder what I would do today, knowing what came of it all in the long run. I recognize now that the church needs an organizational structure and that it is best if we all work together, following the lead of those who have been entrusted with administrative positions. On the other hand, the church will always need visionaries. H. M. S. Richards, J. L. Tucker, William Fagal—all of these men sensed God calling them into new ways of evangelism. None of them had conference support to begin with, but all of them founded ministries that eventually became a part of the organized work.

Was it God's call I heard—the call that prompted me to decide to go off the conference payroll and found an independent ministry called Prophecy

Countdown? I have no doubt that it was God who called me to television ministry. But some of the things that happened after we founded our own ministry—I must admit, with tears in my eyes, that all too often I let another spirit control my decisions. It was that old seed of bitterness that had prompted Walter Rea and others to do things that would wound God's church.

The seed of bitterness was planted in events that came after our decision to go independent. I can honestly say that on the way home from the conference office after Elder Carruba told me I had to decide between conference employment and television evangelism, I didn't feel a bit of anger. I understood that this was the position the conference had chosen to take and that he couldn't do anything but relay that message to me. I respected—revered—the conference leaders and couldn't be angry with them.

At the end of the three-week period, we reluctantly told the conference committee that we were going to continue with our broadcasts and that we would await their final decision as to our employment. They graciously told us that we could remain on payroll until the end of that year—about four months—but from that point on, we were on our own. We were thankful for their support—they had gone as far as they believed they could—and the months that I would continue to receive a salary would prove a genuine blessing as we geared up for our nationwide launch.

Our first Tempo program was scheduled for the first Sunday in November 1984—almost exactly one year to the day from the time we did our first local cable broadcast in Naples. In order to meet national broadcast standards, we had to have better equipment than the local cable company provided, and that meant we needed a new set to film at as well. Dianne has always had a flair for decorating and was at that time operating her own interior design business in Naples. She was delighted when the Bonita Springs church invited her to redo the front of the sanctuary to make it suitable both for a church service and as a television studio.

Of course that meant installing high-powered lights in the ceiling, and that meant we would have a lot of extra heat to deal with. We called in an air conditioning specialist, and he told us that when the church had been built the builders had installed twice the air conditioning capacity that was needed for a building of that size. We were so thankful for the foresight of the people who had provided for our needs before we ever knew of them.

BACK ON TRACK

We contracted with a video production company in Miami to film the programs and produce them on one-inch tape, which was standard for broadcast television. We launched our new ministry in a big way that first Sunday in November. I invited the Heralds singing group to come out to Florida, and we had them do songs to open and close the program.

Word quickly went out among Adventists across the country, and our viewership soared right from the start. There was a lot of excitement being generated. People still loved *It Is Written* and *Faith for Today*, but they sensed that *Prophecy Countdown* was something different. We presented ourselves as a full-message ministry, and I soon earned a reputation as a no-holds-barred evangelist who wasn't afraid to speak our whole, plain truth.

As the end of 1984 approached, we were a bit jittery about going totally independent, but our viewers were proving even more loyal and supportive than we had hoped for, and our financial needs were not proving to be a problem.

I've often been accused of starting an independent ministry for financial gain. Money often served as evidence to us that the Lord was blessing and that we ought to continue on in the course we were following. But I can say very definitely that when we were considering going independent, money did not motivate us to make the decision we did. In fact, if anything could have stopped us from going ahead, it probably would have been concern over where our next paycheck would be coming from. My answer is that only in the final judgment will all our motives be revealed.

During the years that we ran Prophecy Countdown, we did our utmost to maintain a tight financial ship. During our last three years we were audited by an independent auditing firm, and we came out with a squeaky-clean rating. I was not personally in control of any financial matters. I didn't even know the code to unlock the punch locks on the doors to the accounting department in our building.

Dianne and I did draw a salary from the ministry after Dianne closed out her business and came over to serve as president of the ministry. But my salary was, and always has been, less than I would have been receiving if I had stayed on as a conference pastor. And Dianne's salary was in that same modest range. As far as royalties are concerned, Prophecy Countdown policy for the payment of royalties to authors is the same as that outlined by the General Conference policy that was in effect in the 1980 denominational guidelines.

I'm getting ahead of my story, I realize, but it's important to me right now to review the reasons why we did what we did. We honestly felt the Lord leading us into this specialized form of ministry. We were willing to do it, even if we went broke doing so, just as we had been willing to close our business in Avon Park to answer the Lord's call to study for ministry.

Those who criticize us, accusing us of doing it all for money, don't recognize the agony and suffering that we went through in deciding to leave the organized work. They don't know what uncertainties we faced. They don't know that the very house they criticize us for owning was purchased in an extremely distressed situation for only $150,000, which was far below market value, and that it was only by dint of hard labor that we were able to remodel it into the beautiful home that it is today.

I don't mean to be on the defensive, but there have been some extremely painful accusations made against us through the years, and I just wish that instead of spreading vicious rumors and innuendoes and speculations, people would have come to us and asked us how we handled our financial matters. And in saying that, I have to confess that it would have been a lot better, also, if I had maintained the same principles in dealing with the organized church. I have been just as guilty of faultfinding, evil surmising, and criticism as those who have attacked me. For that I am sorry.

We didn't intend our ministry to go that way when we started out, filled with enthusiasm and trepidation, to proclaim the three angels' messages to the world. But we allowed ourselves to dwell upon the mistakes of the church, and we took our eyes off Christ and the mission He has given to the Seventh-day Adventist Church to proclaim the first, second, and third angel's messages to the world.

CHAPTER 11

As of January 1, 1985, Prophecy Countdown was a ministry independent, but supportive, of the Seventh-day Adventist Church. I continued to maintain friendly relations with the pastors in our area and with Elder Carruba. But gradually I began hearing things that bothered me. No, I must admit, they didn't just bother me; they began to eat away at my heart and to make me angry.

I find it difficult to accept that there should ever be rivalries or competition of any kind in the Lord's work. We're all in this together, and we ought to be striving together to get the job finished and go home.

Having said that, I must be forthright and admit that by nature I am a very competitive person. I thought I had put that behind me when I accepted the Lord's call to ministry, but I have to admit there had been times when I had reveled in the level of success God had given me in evangelism. I didn't object when the conference administration held me up as an example of how pastors should be soul winners. It made me feel proud to be at the top of the list in baptism numbers each year. But I chalked it all up to pride in what the Lord was able to do with one who was fully surrendered to His will.

BACK ON TRACK

When we went out on our own, there was a natural reaction among those who stayed with the conference to have a bit of a competitive attitude toward us—a sort of us-vs.-them mentality. But I fully intended to stay on friendly terms. I even attended workers' meetings from time to time. It was there, in conversation with other pastors, that I began to hear reports that planted a seed of bitterness and competitiveness in my heart. Some of my friends told me that one of the administrators had stood up at a workers' meeting and said some rather negative things about me and had concluded by saying, "John Osborne's going to regret this. Just you wait; he'll come crawling back on his knees to us." Another time I heard that he had said, "We're going to crush John Osborne."

It amazed me to hear those reports, but it wasn't just one pastor who was relaying them to me, so I knew they must be true. Being the fighter that I am, I was ready to storm into the conference office and "put the lights out" for that particular individual. But I labored on my knees about it instead, and God gave me the grace to simply commit the matter to Him. Six months later I heard that the administrator in question had resigned as the result of a divorce. Boy, did I feel justified when that happened!

It probably wasn't right for me to feel that way, but I hope you can understand how I took events like that as evidences that God was on my side and that He would fight for me against whatever foes might try to hinder my ministry.

It was little incidents like that that planted certain seeds of bitterness in my heart, and later this predisposed me to begin reacting rather than acting—to begin responding to criticism with criticism instead of maintaining a clear focus on the task of spreading the gospel to all the world. I couldn't see where and how we were going astray at the time. It was such a gradual road that we followed, slowly downhill into the depths of criticism.

Prophecy Countdown had basically taken over the Bonita Springs Seventh-day Adventist Church by the time we went independent, and the members loved it. They were 100 percent supportive of what we were doing.

I pity the poor fellow that the conference sent into that situation to pastor the Naples and Bonita Springs churches. Clearly, the conference expected him to lead out in the spiritual program of these churches and that I would no longer have a major role. But the members would hear nothing of it. They had allowed us to redecorate their church and turn it into a TV studio. They had given up their fellowship room and turned it into offices for Prophecy Countdown. They sensed that something really important was happening here. Suddenly instead of activity for a few hours per week, the church building that they had sacrificed and worked to build was being used every day in the Lord's work. When the new pastor announced his preaching schedule and told them which weeks he would be speaking at their church, they simply said, "No thank you; Pastor Osborne is going to continue to be our preacher."

But at this time there was no conflict with the local conference or even with the pastor. We got along well together, and he simply accepted the will of the congregation and let me continue to function as the preacher at Bonita Springs, while he was the preacher at Naples. Sure, I suppose there was an attitude on the part of the conference administration that "we need to get John out of there somehow," but as long as my messages were good old Seventh-day Adventist messages, supportive of the church, they were willing to look the other way and let things continue.

Shortly after we went independent, I came across the book *Reaping the Whirlwind*, by Joe Crews. In it, that revered Adventist evangelist (head of the Amazing Facts ministry) really took the denomination to task for letting the distinctive teachings of the Seventh-day Adventist Church slip. I also read another of his little books, *Creeping Compromise*, in which he pointed out that by letting even the smallest of standards slip, we were opening the door for greater and greater error to come into the church.

Those two books had a strong ring of truth to me, and I decided to prepare a series of sermons based on their message.

When I first started broadcasting in Naples, I used Kenneth Cox's sermon outlines and text slides as a general guide. Of course, they required some personal preparation time to adapt to my television audience, but I didn't have to start from scratch, and I knew they were messages that had worked to win thousands of souls. I was not opposed to using the research of others as a starting point for developing my sermons.

I don't mean to imply that I never developed sermons of my own from scratch. Certainly I often did that. Working in my office with my secretary, I would go through my subject, deciding what to say, and she would type it out on the word processor and print it out for me to review. In the later years of our ministry, I submitted every video script to our board for review and corrections, and when I preached, this final version would be up on the Tele-Prompter for me to refer to as I preached.

I preached a five-part series based on those books by Joe Crews—it was my first "Straight Testimony" series, and we were totally overwhelmed by the response. The phone calls poured in—people wanted copies of those tapes—so we began producing and selling sets of audiotapes. I have no idea how many sets of those sermons finally ended up in circulation. I know that we produced and sold 10,000 sets, but how many thousands more were duplicated from those originals we will never know.

My message struck a sensitive chord—one that resonated powerfully with the feelings of countless thousands of Seventh-day Adventists. Remember that this was a time of great turmoil in the church. Some have referred to the early eighties as the FDR era in the church—the time when Ford, Davenport, and Rea (Desmond Ford, Donald Davenport, and Walter Rea) dealt a triple blow to the church. Ford challenged the theological and prophetic understandings of the church; Davenport challenged the financial underpinnings through an investment scandal; and Rea challenged faith in the writings of Ellen G. White by producing a book that accused her of plagiarism.

People were longing for reassurance that the good old Seventh-day Adventist message was still true. Many pastors were caught up in the theological confusion of the era, and their congregations were getting watered-down, meaningless sermons, on Sabbath. Now, here was a dynamic young Adventist preacher who wasn't afraid to say what needed to be said, who was willing to stand up and declare unequivocally that the Lord is coming and that Seventh-day Adventists have been called to a high standard of Christian living as a testimony to the world in these last days. I wasn't afraid to point out where error was creeping in or where the church had compromised with the world. It's no wonder that the tapes sold by the thousands.

And I was glad to be known as one who would stand for the right though the heavens fall.

But for that time and place, it was clear that I had the message that many in the church longed to hear. It was not long after I had completed that five-part Straight Testimony series that the president of the student association at Loma Linda University invited me to come out there for a weekend series of sermons.

I spoke in Gentry Gym on Friday evening and was scheduled to speak again on Sabbath morning. A sizable crowd had gathered, and then, just before I went into the pulpit, someone handed me a bulletin from the university church. In the announcement section I read an invitation to the church family to attend a meeting on Sabbath afternoon at three o'clock, when a Roman Catholic priest was going to speak from the pulpit of the University Seventh-day Adventist Church.

I couldn't believe what my eyes were seeing, and when I got up to the pulpit, I let the congregation know what I thought of such a thing. It seemed to me that the church had gone far astray of its mission, if it was willing to allow a representative of Roman Catholicism to speak from a holy pulpit on the Sabbath day, of all things! I spoke out strongly, mincing no words, against what I saw as a clear sign of apostasy in the church. I abandoned my planned sermon and preached a message I called "The Golden Calf," about the time when Moses came down off Mt. Sinai and found the people worshiping a foreign god. I spoke plainly about our human propensity for doing what is popular, as Aaron did when the people demanded that he set up a false system of worship, and I compared Aaron's sin to sins in the church today. I pointed out that Moses came and gave a straight testimony and that this was not popular but that it was right.

My sermon series was taped and duplicated and sent out to the whole world as "The Straight Testimony at Loma Linda." Tens of thousands of copies of those messages went out worldwide, and suddenly I had not just a nationwide television broadcast but a worldwide ministry. Wherever I went I heard people calling me the new John the Baptist, or John the Adventist.

The success of those sermons impressed me with the need of the Adventist Church to get back to its fundamental messages and the eagerness of much of the membership to hear the kinds of messages they remembered from earlier days before there was so much effort put forth to make the church seem more mainstream.

But one of the most difficult lessons I have had to learn in my ministry is that success and accolades are no guarantee that I am going in the right direction. I realize now that the popular acclaim those messages received helped set the tone of my future ministry. By standing up and taking a hard line, I had attracted a vocal and enthusiastic following.

It wasn't that I preached those messages in order to win or hold my following. I preached those messages because I believed every word that I said, and I believed that the words needed to be said. But I did use the acceptance I received as assurance that I was preaching the right message.

But making strong statements about apostasy in the church was not a way to win friends among church administrators, as I soon discovered.

CHAPTER 12

My messages about apostasy in the church struck a resonant chord among many conservative Adventists, but among church administrators the messages were not so well received. Elder Malcolm Gordon, who was now the Florida Conference president, phoned me and cautioned me about being too critical, but I assured him that I was not attacking individuals but simply pointing out the need for revival and reformation in the church. I saw myself taking a role similar to that of Martin Luther, who stood fearlessly for the right in the face of determined opposition from the church hierarchy.

I was certainly not the first independent minister to stand up and point out the sins of the church, but Prophecy Countdown's reach to Seventh-day Adventists through video tapes, and to the rest of the world through satellite television, called a lot of attention to my messages. Soon men like Ron Spear of Hope International, Colin Standish of Hartland Institute, and Ralph Larson, all of whom had a long history of speaking out about problems in the church, were welcoming me into their fellowship. The three of them came down to Bonita Springs in 1985, and we began producing a series of videos called "Adventist Roundtable." As I think back over what we did and said then, it seems to me that we took a rather judgmental position. But we also tried to point the church in the right direction by reading passages from the Spirit of Prophecy.

The old Indian proverb about not judging a man before you have walked a mile in his moccasins is good advice to all who would criticize others' decisions and judgments or draw conclusions about their motives. There are many difficult decisions that administrators have to make, and whichever way they choose to go, there's sure to be someone who can point out a reason why it was the wrong decision, and to wax eloquent in criticism.

I'm not saying that there were no sins in the church that needed pointing out, and I'm not saying that everything we did in calling people's attention to these things was wrong. But the spirit in which we did it was not always right. All of us had suffered some slights or mistreatment by the organized church, and we let bitterness over those issues sour the spirit in which we spoke. Some of what we said would have been better left unsaid. It serves little purpose to hang all the church's dirty laundry out to be gawked at by the curious and the self-righteous.

We maintained an uneasy truce with conference officials throughout 1985 and 1986. We invited Elder Obed Graham, who was now the conference ministerial secretary, to sit on our board of directors and asked the conference auditors to audit our financial affairs. But as time went by, it became clear that once again I was up against the old "two program" problem that had dogged my school days. The conference leadership had one idea of what should be going on, and I had quite a different idea, and it became more and more difficult to work together. This time, though, I wasn't the one who was expelled. Finally, we formed a board of directors that did not include anyone from the conference.

One of the things that caused friction was my insistence that I must be free to speak the truth as I saw it, to speak out against error in the church, no matter whose toes it might step on. This, of course, did not make me popular with higher levels of the church administration, and local leaders no doubt felt considerable pressure to try to bring me under control. But it seemed to me that these leaders wanted to stifle the movement of God's Holy Spirit in the messages I was delivering. And I continued to feel that there were those in administration who still thought it important to try to crush me and my ministry—as though I was in some type of competition with them.

Another sore point centered around the acceptance of tithes from Seventh-day Adventist Church members. This had become a big issue in the church, because the General Conference and the North American Division had come to realize that a lot of tithe dollars were going to support ministries like ours. The issue was raised and discussed at the General Conference Annual Council meeting in 1985. An action was taken stating clearly that Seventh-day Adventists' tithe dollars needed to flow into the organized church and should not be diverted to the support of independent ministries.

I had studied and prayed over this matter after various people had pointed out to me that Ellen White had made some statements about tithing that weren't generally quoted by church administrators. The conclusion I had reached was that we would not actively solicit tithes from Seventh-day Adventists but that on the other hand, we would not question every donation that came in or return any and all that were tithes.

It was at this time, too, that I began to look at the question of who and what constitutes God's true church and to rethink the statements that seem to indicate that the Seventh-day Adventist Church will go through to the second coming of Christ. It was an alluring train of thought, and at that time I could not see where it would finally lead me. In my Sabbath messages I began making a distinction between faithful Seventh-day Adventists and the unfaithful; the tone of my messages made it plain that while I respected many in leadership positions, I certainly didn't consider that election to a position of responsibility in the church qualified one as a true and faithful member of God's remnant church.

Considering the messages that I was preaching, it wasn't surprising that when the conference officials found that they couldn't control me, they chose to distance themselves from me. By the end of 1986, we were a fully independent ministry, with no direct input from the Florida Conference.

But our support base among the lay Adventist population continued growing. In the spring of 1987 we decided to put together a magazine we called *Prophecy Countdown Telecaster.* By then we had a mailing list of 200,000 Adventists that we had accumulated from various sources, and we sent the magazine to each of those addresses.

I came out strongly in that magazine with articles about who and what the church is and the proper use of tithe. I concluded one article about the church with these words: "What becomes obvious is that God's church is not a religious hierarchy, an organization, or bricks and mortar. God's "church" in the last days are the faithful, loyal, and obedient who love Jesus and keep His commandments."

Beneath that paragraph we placed a painting of Martin Luther nailing his ninety-five theses to the church door and a quotation from the Sabbath School Lesson Quarterly: " 'It is our responsibility to study the Scriptures for ourselves, to ask for the guidance of the Holy Spirit, to submit our understandings to those in the church who are able to judge our findings, and then to abide by the decisions of the church in order to maintain the unity of the church.' " Above that quotation we asked in bold type "What Would Martin Luther Think of This?"

It was plain to see what direction I was headed with this reasoning, but it would be several more years before we fully developed a theology that definitely called for a remnant of true and faithful believers to leave the organized Seventh-day Adventist Church and form an organization that would continue the line of God's faithful remnant.

This magazine also included an expanded version of the straight testimony sermon I had given at Loma Linda. Under the title "The Golden Calf," I had preached this sermon to a very receptive audience gathered at a Hope International camp meeting in Eatonville, Washington, in July of 1986. This sermon placed a strong emphasis on the role of the mixed multitude in leading God's people into apostasy and criticized the evangelistic outreach of the church for baptizing people who had very little awareness of what it meant to be a Seventh-day Adventist. I compared my message to that of Moses and Elijah, who stood firmly for the right while the multitudes continued in apostasy. I went on to speak of the scene in Ezekiel 9 where God's servants are sent out to slay all those in Jerusalem who do not sigh and cry over the abominations done there. Then I began to point my finger at various faults in the church and to decry them as golden calves that the people had set up in place of God. I concluded with a call for repentance and reformation among the people gathered there and in the whole church.

A question and answer column in the magazine allowed me a place to answer people's concerns about the stridency of my message and the fact that we had chosen to accept, but not solicit, tithes from church members.

People appreciated that magazine so much that donations literally poured in. We had a hard time keeping up with the mail. When the flood finally died down, we had collected $100,000 in donations beyond the expense of producing and sending out the magazine. Obviously there were a lot of people who agreed with the stand I was taking.

But of course there were those who didn't appreciate that magazine at all. Among these were the members of the Florida Conference executive committee.

Soon a delegation of five lay people from the executive committee called to make an appointment with me. I knew it wasn't going to be an easy meeting, but the firmness of their stand took me by surprise. They came to my office in the Bonita Springs church and sat across the desk from me. "You know, John, we've been very patient and kind with you thus far," the spokesman said. "We've allowed you to continue to use the church property here, even though you are not employed by the conference. We haven't insisted that you relinquish the pulpit to the pastor assigned to it. But we feel that now you have shown your true colors by the statements you published in your magazine. Do you stand behind everything you published there?"

"Of course I do," I replied.

"These are not the statements of a loyal Seventh-day Adventist minister, John. Your attitude of taking tithes that belong to the church and using them in your ministry certainly disqualifies you. Can't we convince you to back down on some of these points?"

"I will not back down one iota from anything I published in that magazine. You may as well settle that in your mind. John Osborne will not be bullied or forced or threatened into compromising one point of the gospel!" I could see where this interview was leading. It bothered me a lot, and I probably was more combative than I needed to be.

"In that case, John, the conference executive committee has instructed us to notify you that you no longer have the right to use of the conference's property, including the Bonita Springs Seventh-day Adventist Church. You must move out of the church immediately."

"That's ridiculous," I responded. "I'm the pastor of this church. The congregation paid for and built this building. They support me 100 percent, and they want me for their pastor."

"The church is conference property, John," the spokesman said. "And we would be totally within legal bounds if we were to go to the sheriff and demand that he evict you from this property. Now, of course we don't want it to come to that, so we will give you a few weeks to comply with our demands. But if you refuse, don't ever think that we will hesitate for a moment to exercise our legal right to have you and your staff physically evicted from this building and the doors padlocked."

I can't say that I was really surprised by the visit, because my ministry in recent months had been tending more and more to criticism of the organized church, the General Conference, the ministers, administrators, everybody. As people discovered that we were willing to publicize the wrongs in the church, we eventually became a sort of clearinghouse of apostasy! We received so many church bulletins and audio and video tapes that we had to hire people to come in and sort through them and separate them according to categories of sins!

I've learned by hard experience through the years that if you go looking for something to criticize, it's a sure thing that you can find it, no matter where you look. But I hadn't yet learned that. I had gotten in with people who enjoyed finding fault with others—straining at the gnats—and I had found that there were a lot of gnats out there in the church. But our biggest mistake, and the one that we continued to make for many years, was to think that because the ministry was blessed financially, we must be doing the Lord's will by devoting so much energy to pointing out the sins in the church. How much better it would have been if we had devoted ourselves to lifting up God's organized, visible, denominated church as well as calling professed believers back to the standards of Christian holiness!

So, we had been doing a lot of negative tapes, and I wasn't too surprised when the conference committee put its collective foot down and said that enough was enough and that we couldn't use conference property to carry on this kind of ministry any longer. But I was taken aback by the harshness of the attitude expressed. I also knew that I didn't have a legal leg to stand on, so it was obvious that we would have to move—and soon. That $100,000 we had in the bank from contributions came in very handy. A couple in Umatilla, north of Orlando, had offered us property where we could set up offices and studios but it took all the money we had in the bank to make the move.

CHAPTER 13

It was in March of 1987 that the Florida Conference executive committee told us we must, at last, move out of the Bonita Springs Church. We were sad to leave the congregation that had welcomed us so warmly and that had given us such a great boost in getting Prophecy Countdown started, but we sensed that the Lord was leading in providing a place for us to go.

It disturbed us a lot to be treated in that way by the conference, but I think it's safe to say that there were no lasting recriminations on either side. When I'd had a chance to cool down after the confrontation in my office, I could see that the executive committee actually had been very patient with us and that they were only doing what seemed necessary to them. Elder Malcolm Gordon was the president at that time, and he was very receptive to continued contact.

In Umatilla, we moved onto the land that had been made available to us, putting our offices in doublewide prefab buildings. We put six prefab units together to create a small church. We hadn't planned to have our own church. We fully intended to join the Mt. Dora Seventh-day Adventist Church. But the very week we made the move, on Thursday, a delegation of four elders from that church came to our offices and informed our staff that they did not want us in their area, but since it was a free country, they couldn't keep us away. They wanted us to know, however, that we were not welcome at their church.

In July, we established the Rolling Hills Seventh-day Adventist Company with about two hundred charter members. Elder Obed Graham came up and helped to organize us as a company. In the Adventist system, a company is usually regarded as a precursor to the formation of a church. A group that wants to meet together in a new locale typically unites into a company, and the conference executive committee assigns one of its pastors to shepherd the new flock. As things progress and the company becomes financially viable and grows in membership, the members can request that the conference accept them as a full-fledged church.

Because I was leading out in the Rolling Hills Company, the conference did not appoint one of its pastors but asked me to serve as the congregation's lay leader. This was a slight departure from normal procedures, but it serves as a good illustration of the level of trust and mutual respect that existed between our group and the conference administration at that time.

We continued on in a very mutually supportive role, with both sides doing their best to maintain friendly relations for all of 1987, 1988, and 1989. Conference officials had spoken to me about my "straight testimony" tapes and urged me not to make any more tapes of that critical nature; I had seen the wisdom of their counsel and agreed to keep to a much more positive tone.

The Rolling Hills Company continued to grow, and I continued to serve as lay leader. I suppose the reason we never appealed to the conference to be made a church was that we enjoyed running our own program and didn't really want the conference involved in appointing a pastor. It was a minor thing, really, but looking back on it, I know that it was a symptom of my old propensity for having to run my own program. I worked well as a conference pastor for more than four years, but now I enjoyed the freedom to move quickly and decisively without having to consult with a bureaucracy.

It was a bit like my experiences in school. There were two programs running in the conference—theirs and mine—but in this case we were able to maintain enough separation that both sides stayed happy for quite a while.

The programs we produced during this time were largely evangelistic in nature, and in August of 1987 we got a slot at 11:00 on Sunday morning on WCPX, the CBS affiliate in Orlando. Signing on with that station proved to be a double blessing, because the station even went so far as to build a set for our production right in its own facility.

Viewership continued to increase, and in the fall of 1989 we worked with the Florida Conference to hold evangelistic meetings in the Central Orlando Seventh-day Adventist Church. Our opening night attendance was four hundred, and the interest held all through the meetings, never dropping below three hundred in the five weeks of meetings. At the end of the meetings we baptized seventy precious souls.

That was a real high point for me—a time when we could see precious fruit from our ministry. We had been independent for nearly five years now, and we had seen good results as far as expansion of the broadcast. Our finances had been up and down quite a few times, but we were getting established on a fairly firm footing. But to see those seventy people being reborn in the Lord made all the hard work and struggles seem worthwhile.

There is one dark blotch on those happy days in Orlando, though, and if I don't mention it, some will feel I have been less than straightforward in this book. So I will briefly relate it to help clear the record, since it has been sensationalized and embellished as it passed from place to place. It was tragic that it had to happen during the evangelistic series and cast its shadow over that glorious time, but the Lord knows He's going to be working with flawed clay when He calls us to be vessels for the gospel. I thank Him and praise Him that He still was able to work through me, despite these unfortunate circumstances.

I don't want to name names. Those who already know the story will know who was involved, and that's all right. I feel no animosity toward the people involved.

Letters of apology and forgiveness have been exchanged by both parties, so to write out a detailed story would not be in keeping with how Christ would handle the situation. But, to briefly summarize that incident, I had an encounter with a terminated employee that turned into a confrontation with each one defending his rights. Neither of us conducted ourselves in a way that was appropriate, and as a result a spiral of retaliation ensued, and the incident became a focus of public attention because of the public position I was in. As I reflect on that time, I see that there were wrongs and misunderstandings on both sides, and I have personally learned some wonderful lessons about how merciful and good the Lord is to us all, in spite of our humanness. How much He loves us!

It was a sad and troubling time for us, but as the evangelistic meetings came to a close and we saw those seventy souls take their stand in baptism, we had every reason to rejoice and celebrate God's goodness to us.

But while we were celebrating that great triumph, others were starting to use the concept of celebration in ways that we did not believe the Lord intended.

And you don't suppose I could just sit idly by and silently watch these new and disturbing developments in God's church, do you?

CHAPTER 14

As you can tell by looking at the cover of this book, I'm writing it in cooperation with Ken Wade, who is a book editor at Pacific Press. Prior to that responsibility, Ken was an associate editor of *Ministry*, our church's publication for pastors, put out by the General Conference Ministerial Association. Ken stayed in our home for several days while we talked about this book, and he interviewed Dianne and me at great length. One morning at the breakfast table he told me an interesting story about visiting a celebration church. Ken knew that I had come down very hard on celebration churches in 1990. At about the same time he had been assigned by *Ministry* to investigate what was happening in the celebration churches and to co-author an article on celebration worship with J. David Newman, the magazine's executive editor.

Ken prefaced his story by telling me about his experience as a pastor in a small church. The children's department leader there had begun to wear some rather flashy jewelry, and the church had had to deal with the issue by replacing her at nominating committee time.

Several years later, Ken was visiting a celebration church on assignment from *Ministry*, just observing what was going on and interviewing the pastor. He said that during the service someone tapped him on the shoulder from behind, and when he turned around, he was engulfed in a big hug by the woman who had been the children's leader at his church.

I interrupted Ken's story by exclaiming "And now she was *really* decked out, right?"

Ken stopped and looked at me for several seconds with a big grin on his face. "No," he replied. "She didn't have on a single piece of jewelry."

"Wait a minute!" I said. "Now, you're really blowing my theory!"

Ken went on to explain that later he'd had a chance to talk with the woman, and she had told him that the jewelry had been important to her there in the little, conservative Adventist church that he had pastored because it helped her establish a positive self-image. She was self-conscious about her weight and just felt the need of putting on something flashy to distract people from her shape. When she and her husband moved and someone invited them to the celebration church, she said she felt so loved and accepted there—just as she was—that the jewelry became unimportant, and she took it off.

That was just the opposite of what I expected. Sometime in 1989 I began to hear about celebration churches, and the reports I got indicated plainly to me that Pentecostalism was moving into the Seventh-day Adventist Church lock-stock-and-barrel. I could plainly see that this invasion was leading us down the road to disaster. Up to this point I had used audiotapes to distribute my sermons, but now I realized that I needed to be able to *show* people what was going on, so we decided to make a two-hour video, just for distribution to Seventh-day Adventists. It wasn't a program that we broadcast; this was something for "in-house" distribution only. We made the video and called it "The Greatest Crisis in the History of Adventism." Copies went out by the thousands, and a lot of people became really concerned about the effect of celebration worship services in Adventism. We heard from a lot of them, and many sent us their own experiences and videos they had shot in celebration services.

That first tape on celebration worship literally went around the world! The General Conference president relayed how that once when he was visiting a little remote village in Africa, he had barely gotten out of the Jeep when a tribesman came up to him and asked, "What about celebration in USA?" Elder Folkenberg didn't know what the man was talking about until he said, "We have video," and held up a copy of that tape I had made.

A layman at the 1990 General Conference session in Indianapolis brought a copy of the video and set up a projector in a hotel room and went out on the streets with placards, inviting people to come in and see what was happening in Seventh-day Adventist celebration churches. A lot of people saw the video there, I'm sure, and many of them ordered copies to share with friends.

I'm still convinced that I was absolutely right in opposing celebration worship in that video. I pointed out clearly from the Bible and from the Spirit of Prophecy that bringing a spirit of raucous celebration into our worship services is wrong, especially in this antitypical Day of Atonement when we should be preaching repentance and conversion and preparation for the Second Coming.

The celebration churches that I had heard about were bringing in rock bands and teaching people to clap their hands and shout and sway back and forth to the rhythm of loud, syncopated music. I had it on good authority, from firsthand witnesses, that speaking in tongues had begun to break out in some of these churches. My staff and I carefully researched the Spirit of Prophecy to see what light the Lord could give us on this situation, and the quotations I used in my sermon made it very plain that the Holy Spirit could not be blessing in this type of worship service. Rather, the people were opening themselves up to a very unholy spirit. They were literally driving the angels of God away by their party atmosphere.

As I prepared that video, I realized that I would have to deal with the questions and objections of those who knew that their pastors and conference leaders were actively promoting celebration worship—not only promoting it but holding seminars in which pastors were brought in to learn how to lead a celebration service. I spoke carefully and judiciously, choosing my words with great tact, but I made it plain that if the leaders were going to take our church down that path, those who stood for right and truth would have to take a stand against them.

That tape went out in February of 1990. In March I heard from Elder Malcolm Gordon, the president of the Florida Conference. Elder Gordon asked me to come down to the conference office. I could sense that the warm relationship we had maintained with the conference for three years was beginning to cool down as a result of that video.

My whole board went with me to the conference office to meet with Elder Gordon and Elder Obed Graham, who was now the conference secretary. These men told me in no uncertain terms that they could not approve of the things I had said on the video about the leadership of the church and that the conference could not maintain a relationship with Prophecy Countdown if we were going to continue to make such tapes. I don't know for sure, but I imagine that they were getting quite a lot of pressure from higher levels in the church to bring me into line.

"We want you to understand," Elder Gordon said, "that this has to be your *last* tape on celebration worship and the sins in the church. If you value your membership in the Seventh-day Adventist Church, you will *not* come out with any more videos like this."

Well, at that point I felt that I had said all that needed to be said on that issue, so I assured them that I didn't have any plans to produce any more videos. We parted amicably, still planning to continue to work together. We had always invited one or more members of the conference committee to meet with our board; we respected and valued the relationship we had with the organized church. We didn't want to do anything to damage that relationship, but on the other hand, I felt strongly called of the Lord to speak the truth as I understood it, without having to answer to the larger organization for everything I said.

I honestly did not plan to do any more videos about celebration churches, but soon we were totally overwhelmed with materials that were pouring in from around the world—stories and videotapes showing what seemed to me *horrible* things going on in our churches, in our youth camps, at our colleges. Conference, union, and even division leaders were participating and promoting things that we could not believe were of the Lord.

I hadn't promised not to make another video. I had simply told the brethren that I had no plans to do so. You've probably figured out by now that I'm pretty open to a change of plans when that seems necessary. In response to all the things we were getting in the mail, I felt compelled to release another video that we called "The Greatest Crisis in the History of Adventism II."

The conference officials weren't interested in my explanation about simply changing my mind. They felt I had broken a promise and that I was totally unwilling to respond to their wishes. Within a couple months of that second video's release, I got word from the conference that I had been removed as the lay leader of the three-hundred-member Rolling

Hills Seventh-day Adventist Company.

The church met in business session to discuss this and voted to send a letter to the conference asking for reasons from the Bible or Spirit of Prophecy why I should not continue as the leader of the company. The letter further stated that if such reasons were not supplied, John Osborne would continue as leader.

There were a number of communications back and forth, but by midsummer it was clear that we could not come to a meeting of the minds. Finally in November of 1990, the conference sent us notice that the Rolling Hills Seventh-day Adventist Company was being disbanded for "failure to recognize properly constituted church authority."

I felt very bad that our relationship had been broken off in that way, but I didn't feel that I should stop what I was doing. The Lord seemed to be blessing us, and we believed that we were preaching His message, so we continued to meet as an independent Seventh-day Adventist congregation.

I continued to produce videos about celebration. Altogether, we produced seven videos, based largely on reports and videotapes we were getting from people who had seen the earlier tapes. Meanwhile, relationships with the local conference went from bad to worse. Communications became more and more acrimonious.

The response my videos were getting from lay people around the world made me feel triumphant, strong, and blessed. But in the depths of my soul that old seed of bitterness was being richly watered, fertilized, and tended. I felt that I had been done dirty, and I was out to prove that I was the one on God's side. Somehow I overlooked everything the Bible says about resolving conflict, because I've never been one to back away from a fight. I convinced myself that I was the wounded party, and it was easy to begin justifying what I was doing and at the same time wound the leaders of God's church. All too often I allowed the worldly spirit of "don't get mad, get even" to permeate my service of the kingdom of God. And I paid a stiff price for my obstinate rejection of church authority. Soon I was informed that if I continued to disregard the guidance offered by conference leadership, my church membership would be dropped.

Accusations and recriminations went back and forth for nearly a year, during which time I continued to feel it important to produce videos about celebration. We weren't producing them for the money's sake, but the funds that poured in as a response helped to validate our position. Since we were a video ministry, it was a sound business decision, as well as a spiritual one, to produce additional videos on the same topic as volumes of additional material came in.

By the fall of 1991 it was clear to me that I was about to lose one of my most treasured possessions—my membership in the Seventh-day Adventist Church. Because the membership of everyone who belonged to the Rolling Hills congregation had been transferred to the Rolling Hills Company in 1987, the actual membership was held in the conference church. This meant that my membership was held at the discretion of the conference executive committee. When it became clear that the committee planned to disfellowship me on the basis of my rejection of its authority, I made arrangements to have my whole family's membership transferred to a small congregation in Montana and asked to be dropped from the conference church.

The Florida Conference executive committee went ahead and disfellowshiped me at the end of September, and two weeks later the Montana congregation accepted me on profession of faith and accepted my wife and son by transfer. This led to a long series of communications between church leadership and the people in Montana, in which the administrators made it clear that the Montana church had not followed correct policy in accepting me on profession of faith after I had been disfellowshiped by a different Seventh-day Adventist congregation.

In the end the small Montana church wearied of the administrative pressure they were receiving on the issue, and Dianne and Johnny and I took our membership, by transfer, to the Angwin, California, village church. Our memberships remained there for several years, but when I finally came to my senses and recognized how deeply I had rebelled against properly-constituted church authority, I realized that I needed to repent of that sin. Although technically I could have simply transferred to another congregation, I realized that I needed to make a public stand, confess my sin, and begin a new relationship with God's remnant church.

While I was producing those videos, I was sure I was right in pointing out the wrong path the church was taking in celebration worship, and I'm still convinced that much of what we said and did was right. But I realize now that I have been too judgmental at times. There are people who have been blessed, as Ken told me, by the spirit of acceptance and forgiveness that was emphasized in some of the celebration services. Some of our churches are so cold, I know. But the method of warming them up was what we strongly disagreed with.

Ken also told me that the same woman who was brought back to a closer relationship with the Lord, and the church, as a result of attending that celebration church now recognizes that that particular congregation has gone too far in bringing the ways of the world into its worship services. She is a faithful member of a regular Seventh-day Adventist church in the community where she now lives.

If I had it all to do over again, would I defy the conference leadership and continue producing videos against their counsel? You know about my impulsiveness and about my penchant for going straight ahead into what I believe is right. I'm not sure I know how to answer that question, but I think you'll gain some further insights into why my answer might be different today than it was back then, as you read on and discover what it was that led me to be rebaptized in 1997 and to rejoin God's organized Seventh-day Adventist Church.

CHAPTER

15

U p to the time we began producing the celebration videos, we had considered Prophecy Countdown to be a single-mission ministry. The Lord called me to be a public evangelist, and we founded our ministry with the idea of taking a full-message Seventh-day Adventist evangelistic series onto the public airwaves. We believed that the ministries at the media center in California were producing good programs, but we felt that we could fill a niche that was being neglected.

It Is Written was presenting the Seventh-day Adventist message to the world, but in what we felt was a *popularized* version. For instance, *It Is Written* did not produce programs that forthrightly pointed to Roman Catholicism as the antichrist power. Its focus seemed to be on winning friends for Adventism—getting people to think of us as an OK group to join.

While I appreciated this approach, I felt the church should also have a program that spelled things out more plainly—especially the prophetic aspects of our message. Also the 1980s were the decade of expansion for cable networks. New cable networks sprang up all over the country, which meant that there were many new stations looking for programming. It was an ideal time to launch a ministry that would not compete with, but complement, the denomination's broadcasts. Remember, too, that this was the time when the Three Angels Broadcasting Network was starting up in Illinois—also as a supplement to what the denomination was doing.

So we had launched our television ministry with a prophetic focus in mind, and we had stuck largely to that agenda. But when we got involved in pointing out the problems we saw in celebration worship, our ministry made a definite and conscious shift. Now we saw ourselves as having a two-pronged ministry. Prophecy was still important. We would continue to proclaim the three angels' message to the world. But we had an additional message for the church. We referred to it as the Elijah message for the church—the straight testimony: Cry aloud and spare not! Show my people her sins!

It pains my heart to say it, but we learned some very important and disturbing things through that experience. It was a sweet experience at first. Oh, how the support poured in when we began pointing out sins in the church! People loved it because many felt they were not listened to or taken seriously by the church leadership. Now they had a voice, a champion for their cause. They shouted Hallelujah and Amen whenever we took the church to task for its failings. And believe me, wherever you have a human organization—jars of clay that the Lord is trying to use as His instruments—it's always going to be easy to find faults and failings to point to.

When our focus had been almost exclusively on preaching the prophetic message of the church, we had some good supporters, but it seemed like we were often limping along from one financial crisis to the next. We had to borrow money from supporters and sometimes had a hard time finding the funds to repay debts on time.

But when we tapped into the mother lode of people's anger, bitterness, and resentment toward the organized work of the Seventh-day Adventist Church, our financial picture significantly improved. Donations large and small came pouring in, and, as I've said before, this affirmed us in our belief that we were following the right course. We were able to purchase a 10,000 square-foot office building, and our Rolling Hills congregation leased a refurbished former supermarket. Membership grew steadily to a peak of seven hundred members, with about three hundred to four hundred in attendance on Sabbath mornings. About three hundred of our members were in other locales and had quit attending their local churches and joined our group in absentia.

In addition to the members who met at Rolling Hills, we encouraged those in other areas who no longer felt comfortable in their local Adventist congregations to form home churches that would meet in homes and watch our church services, first on video and later with live satellite downlinks. At one point we figured we had as many as six hundred independent congregations watching our live broadcasts and using our Rolling Hills program as their Sabbath worship service. Another four hundred groups purchased tapes and used our service the following week in their home churches. We knew of one church in Wyoming with fifty members that used our satellite program every Sabbath.

I guess you could call it the Absalom Syndrome. You remember that Absalom was David's handsome young son who fell out of his father's favor when he took matters into his own hands and killed his half-brother Amnon, who had raped Absalom's full sister Tamar. In a sense, Absalom was crying aloud and sparing not and bringing about justice in response to wrongs done in the royal household (church administration?). But when he took a stand for what he knew was right, it made him unpopular with his father, who probably should have had the courage to stand up and deal with the situation himself.

As a result, Absalom was "disfellowshiped" from the royal household— he wasn't allowed to come to Jerusalem anymore—until General Joab, David's head of the armed forces, devised a scheme that persuaded David to allow his son to return. But then what did Absalom do? He took a seat at the gate to the city, and whenever any disgruntled person would come to Jerusalem to make an appeal to the king, Absalom would call the person aside and hear his case. "Oh, you poor person," he'd say. "If I were king, I'd see to it that you were treated better than that." In this way, "Absalom stole the hearts of the men of Israel," the Bible says (2 Samuel 15:6, KJV).

Once he had gotten the support of all the malcontents in the land, Absalom went a step further. He went down to Hebron—the place where his father had first been crowned king—and began to preach a message that you might title "What Is the True Israel?" He proclaimed that the kingdom God had given his father was no longer the true kingdom and that it was time to establish a more righteous kingdom.

You know the end of the story—the wars that ensued, the tremendous damage that was done to the kingdom. But in the end God saw to it that the rebellion was put down and the kingdom restored to David.

We certainly didn't see it that way at the time, but when we began to turn our focus more and more to pointing out the sins within the church instead of reaching out to those outside the church to lead them into God's kingdom, we were launching ourselves down Absalom's path. We didn't have to go that direction, and we didn't have to keep following the path, but in all honesty, I have to confess that this course felt good to me. I *enjoyed* it. I *enjoyed* catching these guys with their hands in the cookie jar. We would catch administrators and pastors on video doing the very things we had accused them of but that they had denied doing. It made me feel so good to catch them, because in my eyes it vindicated me as the servant of the Lord in showing His people their sins!

When that little congregation in Montana accepted our membership, you wouldn't believe the amount of flak they caught from upper levels of administration—the amount of pressure that was put on them—all because of accepting one individual into church membership. It was very clear to me that there were people all the way up to the top levels of the church hierarchy who had it in for John Osborne. It wasn't just a matter of enforcing church policy. There are thousands, if not millions, of members of the Seventh-day Adventist Church worldwide who aren't living up to church standards. But administrators don't go after them and demand that the congregation either disfellowship them or face being disbanded and kicked out of their sanctuary.

I could see that there was a definite vendetta against me, and I took it personally, and I wasn't about to take it lying down. I fought back, and the harder I fought, the more support I garnered from others who had allowed seeds of bitterness to spring up in their own hearts. Other church members and former pastors who had a bone to pick with the organized church soon started linking up with us. We would produce video series together on topics like "New Age Adventism," "The Jesuit Agenda," and "The Abomination of Desolation for Seventh-day Adventists."

In about 1992 we linked up with another independent Adventist ministry called Steps to Life, under the leadership of John Grosboll. We had often invited John to speak at our camp meetings, and he had returned the favor. Many of the independent ministries up to this time had been tossing about the question: What is the true church? In 1987 our *Telecaster* magazine had an article on that topic that laid the foundation for believing that there might come a time someday when God would have to call His true and faithful remnant out of the Seventh-day Adventist Church.

In 1993 Steps to Life began publishing a magazine called *Landmarks*, which agitated this question a lot more. John Grosboll is one of the deepest thinkers among the Adventist independents, and many of the rest of us who were leading out looked to him as our theologian—the one who could guide our agenda by his study of the Bible and the Spirit of Prophecy. At this time John began promulgating a view of the church that helped to justify our view of ourselves as the only true Seventh-day Adventists left. We saw ourselves as the modern equivalent of the 7,000 faithful ones whom the Lord preserved for Himself when Israel apostatized under King Ahab.

As this view grew in popularity, we began to move closer and closer to the point where we were uniting with Steps to Life and many other independent ministries to issue an official call to all who were faithful "Historic Adventists" to leave the conference churches and be a part of the purified remnant church. We began calling ourselves "Historic Adventists," even naming the Rolling Hills Church and the Prairie Meadows Church "Historic Seventh-day Adventist" congregations. Many of the home church groups followed suit as well.

John Grosboll began preaching a number of sermons regarding New Testament church organization and the necessity of "coming into line." This was followed up by encouraging the formation of an organization called "The North American Council of Historic Seventh-day Adventists," which was represented and endorsed by more than twenty independent ministries and which would ultimately include all the home church groups and individuals who had separated from the conference churches. The charter meeting was held at the Steps to Life ministry in Wichita, Kansas, in July 1993, followed by a meeting at a "Historic Seventh-day Adventist" camp meeting in Santa Rosa, California, in August.

A year earlier, John Grosboll and Ralph Larson set a precedent among the independent ministries by conducting an official ordination service at the Steps to Life camp meeting in which Bob Trefz, Mike Thompson, and I were ordained. This created quite a stir throughout the Seventh-day Adventist denomination as well as in the ranks of the independent ministries.

Just for the record, several months before my rebaptism on July 12, 1997,

BACK ON TRACK

I publicly renounced my ordination as a "Historic Seventh-day Adventist" minister. I removed the title of "Elder" from our weekly church bulletins and publications and resumed using only the title of "Pastor." I have no question that the call of God as a minister/evangelist is still upon me, but I now acknowledge God's chain of command in His organized church. I will not use the title of "Elder" again unless God's church so chooses to bestow it.

In retrospect, I see now that these were the first public manifestations and tangible evidences that we were indeed beginning to form a new organization, whether anyone wanted to admit it or not (see *The Acts of the Apostles*, 18).

This was all couched so cleverly and introduced so subtly through sermons and publications that it was accepted hook, line, and sinker without anyone realizing the enormity of what was happening.

When anyone would ask us if we were starting a new organization contrary to the Lord's counsel in *Selected Messages*, 1:204, 205, we had clever ways of rationalizing the obvious. In essence, I now see we were self-deceived on this point—each reinforcing the twisted theology of the others—that we were all guilty of the very thing that I often applied in my videos to the conference brethren. When anyone tried to pin us down on this, we, too, had become like "trying to nail Jello to the wall."

We had moved from preaching Absalom's message about "What Is the True Kingdom?" to the point that we were ready to go to Hebron and decry the old "kingdom" and establish our own, openly at war with the established church. Declaring that the General Conference were the ones who had "started a new organization"—not us!

What had started out as our attempt to bring reform within the church was now moving to a crisis point—one that would lead to division and continual fighting for years to come if we were to pursue it.

Our experience of crying aloud and sparing not—pointing out people's sins—had begun as a sweet experience as we had seen our support growing by leaps and bounds. But even as we had seemed to be growing and prospering, holes had begun to appear in our support network.

We soon discovered that many of those who were attracted to our ministry were, shall we say, not necessarily the most loyal people in the world. They were people who chose not to submit to the leadership of their local congregation or of church administration at various levels. How could they be expected to show any more loyalty to our organization?

I don't have an actual count, but over the years that we were independent from the Seventh-day Adventist denomination, between twenty and twenty-five individuals who once worked or were affiliated with us eventually spun off and formed their own independent "ministries," many of them just as critical of us as we were of the denomination. Nobody wanted any chain of command. Nobody wanted to submit to anyone else's authority or discipline. Total rebellion, which has now led to anarchy, is the best way I can think of to describe their attitude.

Whenever anyone was disciplined, they would either join another group or set up their own ministry. The same sort of thing was going on in other independent ministries as well, and anytime we tried to set up some sort of accountability or authority, people would shout "popery!"

But we didn't come to understand the full strength of the bitterness in the seeds we had cultivated until we suddenly were pulled up short and came to realize that we had been galloping headlong down a wrong path. I'm so grateful to the Lord that He somehow got my attention before I had to go galloping under an oak tree and get my head caught there like Absalom.

When Dianne and I came under conviction that we had been going the wrong way, we immediately took our stand and announced that unless we could be persuaded that our former path had been right, we were no longer going to use our ministry's resources to criticize and condemn the organized church. Then we began to see for sure what it was that had motivated most of the people who had been supporting our ministry. Then it was that the full strength of bitterness and hatred that had been driving them was turned on us.

But that's getting ahead of the story a little bit. I need to tell you about a couple of other developments so you'll understand how it was that God finally managed to get our attention and get us turned around and headed in the right direction again.

CHAPTER 16

I don't want you to get the impression that once we started our straight testimony emphasis, we lost all our focus on evangelism. That's certainly not true. The "Straight Testimony" tapes that we produced were distributed to our Seventh-day Adventist supporters and were intended for use only within the denomination. Meanwhile we continued to produce our regular Prophecy Countdown television program for broadcast over several different satellite networks, and we also produced a new set of evangelistic series tapes in one-inch format suitable for broadcast. At various times we were on the Tempo, Lifetime, Trinity, Inspirational, and Black Entertainment television networks.

We were on Lifetime for only two months because the cost was prohibitive at $5,000 per program. Some of the networks literally kicked us off for the messages we preached—but these were not messages criticizing anyone. The Trinity network took our slot away from us after I preached on hell— that it did not burn for eternity. One or two other networks also objected to that message; it seemed to bother them a lot more than did the Sabbath message!

There was some enthusiasm for the evangelistic projects among our supporters, but the bread and butter of our financial support came from those who were purchasing and distributing my "Straight Testimony" tapes. I don't want to make it sound like these people weren't interested in evangelism—they were. In 1991 I got word from our media-buying agent that a half-hour slot was available on the SuperChannel in Europe. This is the equivalent of TBS here in the United States—it's on virtually all cable systems throughout Europe. It would cost us $7,000 a week for a half-hour slot. It seemed an impossible figure based on our past experience of trying to raise $5,000 a week to be on Lifetime, but when the opportunity presented itself, the Prophecy Countdown Board felt impressed to move forward in faith, especially due to the political movements we were witnessing and the opening of the former Soviet bloc nations. Therefore, the Board voted unanimously to make a commitment to broadcast on the SuperChannel for one year. We planned then to present this project to our supporters.

When I presented the need to our people in camp meetings and in a brochure, they came through, and we were able to have our evangelistic program broadcast all over Europe for nearly a year. The response was tremendous. At the end of 1992 an independent congregation in Berlin invited us to come over and hold an evangelistic series. Attendance was good, and we baptized twenty-five members into that little congregation at the end of the series. To this day we continue to hear of baptisms that are resulting from that one year of broadcasts on the SuperChannel.

It seemed that the Lord was blessing our ministry wherever we turned, especially evangelistically, and we began to dream of bigger and better things. Wouldn't it be fantastic, for instance, if we could find a way to get our messages out on the satellite networks *live* instead of via tape? We were spending big money every month, using rented equipment from an Orlando production studio. So we began to look into establishing our own production studio and satellite uplink.

In the meantime, our relationship with the organized church was becoming more and more tense. If you listen to my program tapes through the years, you'll notice a change of tone as you move into the nineties. Prior to that you can recognize a note of genuine concern, even in tapes that criticized aspects of the church. But as time progressed, my sermons became more and more strident, with less and less genuine love and concern expressed. It would be hard for me today to sit and watch some of those tapes.

We've taken all of the critical ones off of the market, but they continue to circulate. We refer to them as toxic waste—they're out there, still poisoning the environment. They won't just disappear.

By 1992 we were basically involved in all-out war with the church administration, and we weren't the only ones firing shots. Someone in the administration of the North American Division got the idea of collecting information about a number of the independent ministries that were causing the worst problems for the church. The church leaders could see millions of dollars in tithe funds being siphoned out of church coffers, and they were continually dealing with all of the accusations that various ministries were leveling at them, so they decided to strike back.

One way of striking back was to begin to put pressure on various levels of the church organization to deal with people who were involved with the independents by making it clear that they could not continue to hold membership in the regular church while involving themselves in such critical activities. By now the war wasn't being fought only at administrative levels. Many local congregations had been split right down the center aisle when some of the members became involved with independent ministries.

When the congregations would appeal to the local conference office for advice, oftentimes they were encouraged to take the bull by the horns and to disfellowship those who were regarded as troublemakers. Other times the people who were involved with independent ministries would walk out of the local congregation themselves and establish their own group, often meeting in someone's home and playing a tape of a sermon from one or another of the independent ministries.

Those of us who were leading out in the independent ministries were very aware of this trend, and it occurred to us that the best way to provide spiritual leadership for the people who were establishing their own home churches would be to form a sort of satellite church network. If we could uplink our programs directly to satellite, then those independent congregations could purchase satellite dishes and take part in live broadcasts from Prophecy Countdown and other ministries.

But more important than that, we recognized from our experience with going on the SuperChannel that our people get really excited about the idea of taking our evangelistic message to the world. When they are presented with opportunities that they can get excited about, they bring their wallets with them and provide the necessary funds.

We had experimented with live uplinks for two Sabbaths back in 1990. We rented production equipment and a mobile C-band satellite uplink truck, brought them out to our church, and provided live programming all day long. We set up a bank of phones to receive calls and heard from about 350 Adventists who had tuned in. It surprised us to discover how many Adventists had satellite dishes, and we knew that the number was growing all the time because of the success of the Three Angels Broadcasting Network.

The success of our mission to Europe was all the encouragement I needed to persuade me that now was the time to move ahead with direct satellite uplink. As soon as we returned from Europe, our board met and agreed to place an order for a mobile C-band uplink truck and mobile production truck from Shook Electronics in San Antonio, Texas. Total cost of this equipment was $1.2 million, but we were confident that our faithful Adventist laypeople would see the merit of having our own equipment for a live satellite ministry. So we moved out in faith, waiting to see how the Lord would provide.

We couldn't have anticipated what happened next. And as I look back on it now, it still amazes me. The Lord knew that our ministry had both positive and negative aspects to it. The Lord was working through the organized church as well, but not everything done there was totally according to His plan either. Through it all, He was blessing both of us, and as it turned out in the long run, what happened finally turned out to be instrumental in bringing Prophecy Countdown back into harmony with the church. But at the time it had the exact opposite effect—it led to some of the most acrimonious exchanges ever between myself and the church administrators.

Those in the church administration who had been collecting information about the independent ministries made a decision to pull together what they had gathered and publish it as a book. That book, titled *Issues: The Seventh-day Adventist Church and Certain Private Ministries*, included reviews and comments on various independents. Materials related to Prophecy Countdown comprised nearly one-fourth of the book (104 of the 467 pages). Included in this material were letters from several former Prophecy Countdown employees who had become disgruntled over disciplinary or other matters and who had vowed to get even with us. The people who put the book together never checked with us to find out if what these angry people wrote against us was true.

That was wrong, because they published a lot of false accusations. But then, I must admit that I had not always done my utmost to let those whom I accused of wrongdoing explain themselves before I produced materials condemning them either. Turnabout is not fair play. Neither of us should have done what we did.

I'm not sure what that *Issues* book accomplished for the North American Division, but I do know what it did for us. When our supporters, and many who had never supported us before, learned about that book and the false accusations it included, they rallied around us as they never had before. The book came out just in the middle of our major fund-raising drive for Caleb (the mobile production unit) and Joshua (the C-band uplink truck). Within two months of the publication of *Issues*, we had raised $800,000, and many of those who made large donations told us that the unfairness of the book had angered them and been part of what encouraged them to be so generous.

Boy, did that make me feel vindicated!

Boy, did that make me feel justified in my anger at church leadership!

We got those trucks in mid-1993 and immediately started putting them to use to broadcast camp meetings sponsored by our network of independent ministries. I stood in front of those beautiful new cameras linked to that fantastic tool of mass communication linked to a satellite 23,000 miles up in space and downlinked to hundreds of Adventist homes all over the country, and I gloated. I looked into the camera with a smirk and taunted the leadership of the Seventh-day Adventist denomination. I told them, "We need another million dollars! Please come out with another *Issues* book—part two!" I justified it all by calling it righteous indignation—just like Elijah on Mt. Carmel.

What pride, what arrogance, what fruit of the seed of bitterness!

CHAPTER 17

The plant of bitterness was now in full fruit and spreading its seeds to the four winds. But even while we criticized and condemned the leadership of the church, we continued our interest in spreading the gospel to all the world. We continued to see ourselves as having a dual mission, and our eyes were blinded, as it were, to the source of the critical spirit that caused us to paint the problems of the church in the worst possible light. In Revelation Satan is called the "accuser of our brethren" (12:10, KJV), and now, unbeknown to us, we were playing that role even while we continued our prophecy-centered outreach ministry.

We were able to justify this course in our minds by referring to the ministry of men such as John the Baptist, Isaiah, Jeremiah, and Elijah, who all cried out against the sins done among God's people even as they pointed forward to the first coming of Christ. But I didn't realize how smart Satan is. He's had thousands of years of experience as the accuser, and he knows just how to point out sins and how to motivate people to dwell on those sins instead of on Christ, who is the Saviour from sin. And if we allow even one little seed of bitterness to have a place in our hearts, Satan knows just how to cultivate it and to make us feel like we are doing the right thing when we let it flower and spread its seeds all around us.

And, of course, we attracted people to us who were motivated by the same spirit. They were honest, sincere souls in many ways but equally unaware of the way that bitterness was blinding their eyes.

In 1991 I met Bob Trefz, a man who seemed very sincere and devoted to the truth. He had spent years researching material related to various conspiracy theories and had come to the conclusion that our church was being led down a wrong doctrinal path by Adventist scholars who had gone to secular universities and universities sponsored by other denominations.

Bob came to Prophecy Countdown, and we taped a number of programs together under the title "The Jesuit Agenda." Bob became more than a resource person for us; he became a close personal friend. Through the years, Dianne and I have learned that it is important to keep our private lives somewhat separate from our ministry lives. Not many people have ever been invited into our home or invited to go on a vacation trip with us, but Bob and his wife were kindred spirits in many ways. After one particularly hectic taping session in early November 1993, we decided to take some time off and go to Jamaica together. Ralph Henderson was another close friend at that time. He and I had been singing together and producing cassettes and CDs. Ralph and his family joined us also. Jamaica was a place that Dianne's family had visited often when she was growing up, so it was a natural destination for us when we needed some time to relax and recuperate.

One morning while we were there, Bob came to breakfast looking really disturbed. I asked if everything was all right, and he said he had hardly slept at all the night before. "The Lord woke me up every hour on the hour," he said. "I couldn't quit thinking about the power of shortwave radio for spreading the gospel. Finally at two o'clock this morning, the Lord spoke to me and said, 'Tell John Osborne about shortwave radio.' Do you know anything about shortwave radio, John?"

When I told him I didn't, he went on to explain that all over the world millions of people have shortwave radios to tune into broadcasts from distant countries. Europe and America are dominated by television and FM and AM medium-wave radio. But in almost every other area of the world shortwave radio is the people's choice because the signal travels much farther than other forms of broadcasts. A person living in a little hut in the depths of the African jungle can easily pick up signals from the United States or China or just about anywhere else in the world.

As Bob talked, I began to think of the possibilities. We already were reaching America and Europe with satellite television. But from what Bob was saying, if we wanted to reach the rest of the world, shortwave was the obvious way.

The idea of reaching the world with shortwave radio lighted a new fire in me. Ever since I first heard the call of the Lord to be a public evangelist, I've had what seemed like a fire in my bones for spreading the gospel to all the world. If we could find a way to use shortwave radio, the *all the world* portion of my vision would be closer to fulfillment.

Later that day I called our office and asked to speak to the engineer who was in charge of our satellite uplink. "Do you know anything about shortwave radio?" I asked.

"Do I!" he exclaimed. "I've been interested in shortwave broadcasting for twenty years. I've studied it a lot. In fact, when Adventist World Radio was looking for a chief engineer for their station on Guam, they almost hired me but decided on another man since I wasn't working in shortwave right at that time."

"Well, praise the Lord," I responded. "He was saving you for us!"

"What do you mean?" he asked.

"Are you sitting down?" I responded.

"Yes."

"The Lord has laid a burden on my heart for shortwave radio. One way or another, we need to find a shortwave station that we can use to broadcast the three angels' messages to all the world."

"What would you like me to do?" he asked.

"Do you know of anyone who could help us to find a shortwave station we could buy or rent or get air time on here in the United States?"

He told me that he had a very good friend who was a real expert in shortwave radio and that if anyone would know of a station for sale, he would. "But why limit our search only to the United States?" he asked.

"Because we need some way to link our satellite TV broadcasts directly into a shortwave signal for the rest of the world," I explained.

To make a long story short, our engineer contacted his friend and learned that one of the finest shortwave stations in all the world had been put up for sale *just that very week!* His friend was acting as the agent to sell the station, and he had received the prospectus just the day before—the very day that Bob kept having dreams about using shortwave to spread the gospel.

Needless to say, when we learned about this station coming up for sale at precisely the right time for us, we sensed the Lord's leading once again and decided to proceed as quickly as we could to try to acquire it as an additional outlet for our programming. It seemed to us that miracle after miracle occurred to facilitate the process, and within a few days we took our corporate officers up to Bangor, Maine, to see the station and to try to negotiate a deal to purchase it.

The station had been built in 1987 by the Christian Science Church at a cost of $7.2 million dollars. The agent told us that it was in an excellent location and that its 500,000-watt signal could reach all of Europe, including western Russia and the Middle East and all of Africa. We had tested the waters a bit with our supporters and learned that it wouldn't be hard to generate a lot of enthusiasm for purchasing the station, so we felt comfortable offering $4.5 million for it. At this time we were working closely with four other ministries, and with our combined fund-raising ability, we didn't feel that price was out of line at all for a facility that could reach so much of the world.

We spent the morning meeting with the Christian Science leaders, but by lunchtime we hadn't made much progress. They didn't feel they could accept anything less than $5 million, and we had agreed that we would not offer more than $4.5 million—for us it was a way of leaving the issue in the Lord's hands. We figured that if He wanted us to have the station, He would help us get it for that price.

We broke for lunch, and each group met to discuss the morning's lack of progress. When we met together after lunch, the chairman of the station's board spoke first. "As you can imagine, there are several organizations that would like to purchase this station," he said. "But we believe that it ought to remain with some sort of Christian group, so we would like you to have it. But we still cannot accept anything less than $5 million for it."

Our faces fell, but then he continued. "However, we have a counter-offer that may appeal to you. We understand that it will take you some time to raise the funds for the purchase. We are prepared to offer you the use of the station prior to the transfer of ownership. In fact, we will offer you free air time valued at $500,000, if you agree to our price of $5 million."

How could we turn down an offer like that? It was definitely a win-win situation. The owners were getting the price they needed, and we were getting the price we needed. Better yet, we had the opportunity to go on the air even before we could raise the full purchase price. Our board voted unanimously to accept the deal, and we went home to start raising five million dollars.

It may sound like a crazy pipe dream to you, but I had learned in my thirteen years of ministry that when you set a dream before people—a dream that involves spreading the gospel—they will provide the funds needed to turn the dream into reality.

We had just finished raising over one million dollars to purchase Caleb and Joshua, and with those two trucks, our ability to communicate with our scattered flock of independent churches had multiplied. More important, over the past two years a loose affiliation of five ministries had begun to take shape under the rubric of the Historic Adventist Movement. The ministries that we worked most closely with were Steps to Life, headed by John Grosboll; Biblical Studies Institute, headed by Bob Trefz; Printed Page Ministries, headed by Les Balsiger; and Modern Manna, headed by Danny Vierra.

Prophecy Countdown was the most visible, most widely known of these ministries because of our television ministry, but the others were all led by powerful speakers with a strong reform message. We saw ourselves as a union of reformers—a group of leaders who had been called especially by God to cry aloud and spare not, to point out the sins in the church, and to call the faithful to a renewed dedication to high standards and vigorous evangelism to prepare a people for the Second Coming. We felt that the church had failed in its mission, that it was compromising with the world, and that God needed us to bring about a reformation just as Martin Luther and his colleagues had done in the sixteenth century.

Each of our groups held a camp meeting at least once a year, and this gave us an opportunity to be together, because we would invite each other to come and speak. As soon as we got Caleb and Joshua operating, we began going from meeting to meeting, feeding the proceedings direct to our satellite network. Many Adventists already had satellite dishes to pick up 3ABN broadcasts, and when we started doing live uplinks, the word went out, and hundreds more purchased dishes to allow themselves to participate in our camp meetings and church services.

Our ability to minister and to reach people was growing by leaps and bounds. We had a wake-up call for the world. And now we were equipping ourselves to spread it to much of the world. But what we didn't realize was that we were moving forward at juggernaut speed to an encounter with God's wake-up call to us!

CHAPTER 18

For quite a few years we had seen nothing but the Lord's blessing wherever we turned in our ministry. Sure, problems had arisen. People had come to work with us and had gotten disgruntled with our leadership and had moved on to form their own ministries or had gone to join another independent group and had turned their critical spirit against us. But we had weathered all the storms and stayed afloat.

We had been growing stronger and stronger and had learned to focus on the positive evidences of God's blessing and leading. But as the ministry grew larger, with more details to attend to, it became like many other churches and ministries. Our administrative team was kept so busy keeping the ship afloat and moving that there really wasn't adequate time to stop and consider whether we were on the right course.

We were headed into a gale at full throttle. Soon we would be compelled to reconsider our course.

Things started out well as we began raising funds to purchase the radio station. We signed the purchase agreement on November 23, 1993. Four days later we held a telethon at Hiawassee, Georgia, which we uplinked to satellite. By this time we had our own satellite network called the Prophecy

Countdown Television Network. We would normally broadcast for four hours on Sabbaths, but we were moving toward being on the air twenty-four hours a day with religious, health, and educational programming.

We took Caleb and Joshua, our production and satellite uplink trucks, to Hiawassee for a weekend of spiritual meetings. During these meetings we announced the purchase of the radio station in Maine. The response was overwhelming as we asked the viewing audience to call in their pledges. We planned to rename the station WVHA (World Voice of Historic Adventism) as soon as we were able to take possession of it. It took us only two hours to raise a quarter of a million dollars for WVHA.

When our supporters caught the vision of what the station could do, they were generous almost beyond our greatest dreams. Within two months we had raised two million dollars! On January 17, 1994, we went on the air with our first shortwave broadcast, taking advantage of the half million dollars in free air time the owners had thrown in to sweeten the deal.

Our total costs for acquiring the station would run around $5.5 million because of licensing and other fees added onto the purchase price, but by February 1994 we were more than a third of the way there. We honestly believed that we would have the full purchase price in hand within six months, which was the amount of time we had told the station's board we would need to raise the money.

Our coalition of five ministries was working well together—united behind the idea of spreading the gospel to all the world but held together by the suspicious, critical spirit that we shared.

On February 6 an exodus of three vehicles pulled away from Prophecy Countdown headquarters. In the lead was Moses—our recently purchased fifteen-passenger van—pulling behind it a trailer with a backup generator to power Caleb and Joshua. They crossed the country in three days, and we set up our equipment at the Orange Show Pavilion Center, a five-thousand-seat auditorium in San Bernardino where we had scheduled a camp meeting and also nightly telethons to raise funds for WVHA. We anticipated raising a million dollars in three days, starting on Wednesday, February 8.

Bob Trefz, Les Balsiger, John Grosboll, and Danny Vierra were already there when we arrived. They welcomed us, but there was a certain coolness in their greetings. Later as I thought back on it, I realized that our reception hadn't been as enthusiastic as I had expected.

We began our meetings on Wednesday evening, but unbeknown to us, trouble between our various ministries was brewing in the wings. We now refer to that meeting as the San Bernardino Ambush, or as our Tower of Babel experience.

There was a strange foreboding in the air Wednesday evening when the other ministry leaders were noticeably absent from the telethon prior to the meeting. The reason for their absence became evident on Thursday morning during a break between meetings. Dianne and I had been up front, and when we went off stage for the break, John Grosboll came up to me and told me that all the other ministry leaders wanted to meet with us in a minivan out in the parking lot. I could tell by the way he spoke, even the way he walked, that something was wrong, but I had no idea just how wrong until we got to the van.

When we were all together, John Grosboll was the spokesman. He explained how the four of them had been talking a lot about the finances for the station. He told us they had concluded that we needed to make some new financial arrangements for the ownership of the station. "We are concerned that it is placing too much control of the funds in one ministry's hands when we're all contributing to the fund-raising effort," he said.

I glanced at my watch. Fifteen minutes of a planned twenty-minute break had passed. John was scheduled to be the next speaker. "What are you suggesting we do, John?" I asked.

"We need to rework the agreement so that all of us have part ownership in the station. We just need your agreement right now that we will rework the ownership so that we all have some control of the station."

"That's not what we agreed on," I responded. "We agreed that Prophecy Countdown would hold the legal documents and that all the other participating ministries would have free air time. I just don't see how we can change that. Our ministry's name is on all the legal papers, the licensing applications, everything. I can't see going back and starting over again on all of that."

John was looking at his watch now. "I have to go, John," he said. "I'm next up to speak. I'll let the rest of you work this out between you."

With that, he got up and headed for the auditorium. Dianne and I sat in stunned silence, looking from face to face, seeing only firmly set jaws. Obviously this group had prepared for this confrontation, and they formed a united front against us. I tried negotiating, reasoning, pleading for time to think it over, every tack I could, but to no avail. The other three were with John Grosboll. They told us that they would not participate in any further fundraising unless we backed down and agreed to share ownership of WVHA.

I didn't understand why at the time, but somehow I just knew for sure that what they were proposing was not right for us. Somehow I sensed that God had placed that radio station in Prophecy Countdown's hands, and as Dianne and I talked and prayed over the situation, we could not see our way clear to back down. We had to stay the course, even if it meant sailing alone.

We left that parking-lot meeting without any solution. We held firm, and so did they. Needless to say, people soon sensed that something was wrong in Historic Adventism. The program wasn't going along as announced. Prophecy Countdown was the only ministry represented during the telethon portion of the meetings. We didn't explain the problem at the time, but people couldn't help but recognize that some sort of rift must have developed in the union, and the pledges that came in didn't anywhere near meet our expectations.

We closed up shop after the last meeting on Saturday night, exhausted and discouraged. We would later come to call that meeting our Tower of Babel experience. But we didn't yet realize how much confusion lay ahead.

CHAPTER 19

There's an old saying, "There's no honor among thieves." I suppose the corollary to that might be, "There's no praise among accusers."

We had been playing the role of accusers of the brethren, and we had fallen in with a band of accusers. We hadn't carefully considered what might happen if ever we had a falling-out with such a band. We soon found out.

Letters and magazines poured from the mimeographs and presses of our former friends, full of explanations of what had happened in San Bernardino and full of accusations about Prophecy Countdown.

Now, suddenly the tables had been turned on us. We, a small, upstart ministry, had been having a heyday tilting at the windmills of the big, bloated, rich General Conference of Seventh-day Adventists. But in the blink of an eye we had now been transformed, in the view of our opponents, from the little guy fighting the giant into the big organization that was robbing tithes and offerings from the smaller groups!

Over the next twelve months the rift that had developed at San Bernardino widened into a chasm filled with harsh words, judgmentalism, backbiting, and evil surmising. What had started out as a wonderful union with intentions of fulfilling the evangelistic branch of our ministry had been cut down and hacked to pieces by the other branch—the critical branch. Criticism is a two-edged sword, and that's why Jesus warned us not to judge lest we be judged with the same judgment we have measured out to others.

The Lord now allowed us to go through months of burning at our own stake, as it were. As each of the ministries involved in the coalition began hurling fiery darts at us, and sometimes at each other, financial resources disappeared like rain on the sands of the Sahara.

We didn't understand what was going on at first, but just a few weeks after the San Bernardino Ambush, I began to realize that perhaps this was the Lord's hand of chastisement upon us because of our critical spirit. I preached one sermon, in April or May, I believe, in which I referred to what happened there as a Tower of Babel experience that the Lord had used to confound the independent ministries.

But you can't turn a battleship around on a dime, and we were so involved in crying aloud and sparing not, pointing out sins in the church, that we couldn't stop and change direction overnight either. I may have realized that the Lord was trying to get us to change course, but I wasn't convicted that He meant for us to swing around one hundred and eighty degrees!

For the rest of 1994 and into the beginning of 1995, we tried to keep going in the direction we had been following, maintaining our dual ministry of evangelism and reformation. And what marvelous results the Lord gave us in our evangelistic outreach, especially through the radio station! Letters began to pour in by the thousands from all over Europe, and especially from Africa, from listeners who were thrilled with the messages we preached. Whole churches, and even districts of churches, were listening in and changing their day of worship. Based on the number of responses we were getting, it was estimated that there must have been as many as ten million people listening to our programs.

And in this success the Lord began communicating with us, too, about our relationship to His church. Our success was creating new problems for us. A pastor in Africa, convinced of the Adventist doctrines we preached, wrote to us, telling us that he wanted to convert and bring his church into the worldwide sisterhood of Seventh-day Adventist churches. But what could we tell him to do? We couldn't send him to the local mission office. If they found out he had been converted by listening to

John Osborne and the other independent ministers that we broadcast on WVHA, the mission officers wouldn't want to have anything to do with our converts. How on earth had we gotten to this place!

In the months following the San Bernardino rally, different ministries eventually joined up with us until we now had six ministries working together. It's interesting to note that the ministries that were so united at the San Bernardino Ambush separated from each other in a relatively short period of time, each pursuing its own agenda.

In 1992, John Grosboll picked up where the Prophecy Countdown *Telecaster* article, "Who and What Is the Church?" had left off. He continued to lead us down the path where we continually focused on that question. It was natural for us, as we dwelt on all the problems in the General Conference, to move toward the conclusion that that organized church certainly was not God's chosen remnant church. But most of our study on this question was based in the writings of Ellen White, and we knew that she had written pointedly that no new organization should be formed (see for example *Selected Messages*, 1:204, 205).

However, where there's a will there's a way, and we had reasoned and rationalized our way around that thought by declaring that under no circumstances would we form a new organization. That would not be according to God's plan. Our mission, we declared, was not to form a new church organization but simply to point out that God's old organization—represented by the General Conference of Seventh-day Adventists—had apostatized back in the fifties in an attempt to find favor with the worldly churches. They, then, had been the ones to form the "new organization." We, on the other hand, who represented the *Historic* Adventist Movement, were actually the continuation of the original Seventh-day Adventist Church, and as such, it was our duty to call people to leave the apostate church and come into God's remnant church.

San Bernardino and what followed was a setback, but it wasn't enough to stop us. We pressed on, continuing to study this issue of who and what is the church.

It was a dangerous question for us to study, and we realized it, but we didn't see where the true danger lay. The real problem with our addressing this question was that we were all too willing and ready to fulfill the role of God's true church, if only we could find justification for declaring that the mainline organization was disqualified. We couldn't take the position of impartial judges. We had too much to gain or lose, based on how we would answer the question. And so our answer was naturally biased.

As we continued to study and ask for guidance, God was listening. But He knew *we* weren't ready to listen, so He allowed us to continue on our path. But He was kind enough to throw some obstacles in our way that forced us to slow down a bit.

We were moving slowly, taking each step carefully, when we decided that we could delay no longer. We decided that in April of 1995 we had to take the final step—issue the official declaration—and give the call to all God's true and faithful people to break off their relationship with the General Conference. It was time to call God's people out of Babylon to join with us in continuing the work of God's *Historic* Seventh-day Adventist Church.

Others had been pressing us toward this ultimate step for a long time, and now finally the six ministries that formed the new coalition agreed that Sabbath, April 15, 1995, would be the day when we would issue the loud cry, calling God's people away from General Conference churches to unite with us in carrying on the true Seventh-day Adventist Church of history. We planned a joint camp meeting in Pennsylvania and let it be known far and wide that all who could should come and that as many others as possible should watch on television because there would be a very big, very important announcement regarding the call out of Babylon.

In all of this the Lord had allowed us to proceed at our own pace—finding our way around the obstacles that slowed us down. But by April He must have realized that it was a now-or-never situation.

I have tried and tried to find out who brought a copy of that little pink book, *The Remnant Church*, into Caleb's editing studio. No one who had access to the truck can remember ever seeing it there before the day I picked it up and started reading as I waited for an editing session to begin.

The other obstacles we had encountered had been as little stones thrown into the path. That book was a brick wall. There was no way to keep on going the way we had been, unless we were willing to smash our way through the revealed will of God and continue on a path He had forbidden.

CHAPTER

The night of April 3, 1995, seemed like the longest night of my life. I knelt beside our bed, praying and crying out to the Lord, seeking light to carry us through the darkness that seemed impenetrable. From time to time I would get up and pace back and forth, talking to myself, thinking things through, trying to come to some sort of rational decision. Where could we go from here?

The things I had read that day had convinced me that I had been traveling down a wrong road. Worse yet, I came to realize that the Lord had forewarned His church, through Ellen White, that people like me would come and lead others astray. At the beginning I had felt that I was fulfilling prophecy by crying aloud and sparing not and pointing out sins in the church, but I had finally allowed bitterness to bring me to the place where I began fulfilling a totally different prophecy by calling people away from the church God had established on earth to proclaim His last-day message to the world.

You know by now that when I come under conviction that I ought to do something, I can't sit still and just think about it. Sometimes my hastiness to act has caused problems because I haven't taken the time to work things through carefully or I haven't been willing to listen to the counsel of others.

So now I was tempted to rationalize. Maybe I was overreacting. Maybe I was being impulsive again. Maybe if I would take more time to study, pray, and counsel with others, I would find out that we hadn't been wrong after all, and we could continue with business as usual.

Every time I would start to feel that way, though, one of the statements from that little pink book would come to mind again, and I would see clearly that we had to change direction—drastically. When morning came, I knew I had to share with our board the things that Dianne and I had been reading. We called together all the board members as soon as we arrived at the office. They could tell, just by looking at me, that something was very wrong.

As I stood up to speak, a heavy sense of responsibility weighed on my shoulders. I had led these people. And I had led them in the wrong direction. I had thought of myself as a Caleb or a Joshua or even a Moses, but in reality for the past few years I had been playing the role of rebellious Korah or one of the men who led the people off to try to conquer Canaan on their own against God's directives.

Somehow I had to redeem the situation. Somehow I had to turn things around and bring the board back with me. I knew that they might turn on me. It was fully within their power to declare that I was now being misled and that Prophecy Countdown would have nothing to do with me or my new message. If this meeting went badly, I could lose everything I had worked so hard to build up. Worse yet, I could lose everything, and the ministry would continue on its wrong path.

Even if the meeting went well and the board elected to accept what Dianne and I had found in *The Remnant Church*, we all still stood to lose everything we had worked for. The ministry itself was in jeopardy. How could we hope to maintain a firm financial footing if we changed our tune and started being positive toward the General Conference?

We began the meeting by kneeling to pray for guidance as we always did. But I can't remember a time when my prayer was more heartfelt. We had made multimillion dollar decisions in that boardroom, but millions of dollars paled in significance when I considered the millions of souls who might be affected by what we faced this day.

After our season of prayer closed, I stood up and looked at the five individuals who, along with me, made up our in-house board. Kathleen Greenfield, our board chairman, sat at the end of the table on my right. To my immediate right was Patti Edwards, our treasurer. On my left, at the other end of the table, sat Dianne, and next to her sat Pat Shafer, my administrative assistant and board member. Across from me were the two associate pastors of our church, Bill Hughes and Dr. Al Scott. They all looked at me expectantly, realizing I had something weighty to share with them.

I looked at Kathleen. Concern was reflected in her dark eyes. I felt like she could see right through me and know the thoughts that troubled me. I wondered how she would respond. Would she understand? Or would she try to take the board with her and continue on the path we had been following?

What about Dr. Scott? A retired orthopedic surgeon, who we affectionately call "Doc," he is a warm, concerned, caring physician. He had been deeply wounded and disfellowshiped by a church in Arizona, and he had proven himself a worthy warrior against those who had done him wrong. A former army major, his caring nature translated into anger when he felt he had been done dirty. Would he be able to turn again and seek reconciliation with those he felt had turned against him?

My other associate pastor, Bill Hughes, had once been a pastor in the Northern California Conference. He, too, felt that he had been handled unfairly by the organized church. How would he respond to my call to return and make amends?

Patti Edwards, the treasurer, seemed mystified. She didn't know just why the meeting had been called and sat expectantly, waiting to learn what was so urgent. It wasn't unusual for some new development to demand a quick board session, but I could see that she sensed the tension in the room as well and seemed a bit apprehensive. A woman of prayer and honesty, I felt that I could count on her to at least give me a fair hearing. And there was Pat Shafer. As I looked at her, I knew I could depend on a sincere, honest evaluation.

I was glad that Dianne was beside me. She knew where I stood, and I knew I could count on her for support.

I took a deep breath and came right to the point. "I don't know how you are going to react to what I have to say today. You may bolt. You may turn against me. You may never want to have anything to do with me again. And if that is the case, I will have to understand. But I am compelled to say what I have to say. I am under conviction, and you know that when the Lord points me in a direction, I just have to go that way."

Alarm showed on the faces around the table as I continued.

"Dianne and I have spent a very long night in prayer," I said. "Yesterday I inadvertently found a copy of the book *The Remnant Church*, by Ellen White, and read it. I have to admit that some of the things in that little book caught me by surprise, even though I know I had read them before. Somehow I had conveniently forgotten what the Lord's messenger has to say about His church. But I can't ignore it any longer. There is no way I can get around it. The Spirit of the Lord has declared that any messenger that declares that the church that keeps the commandments of God is Babylon is deluded and 'will come to nought' (*The Remnant Church*, 45, 46).

"Do you understand what this means? It means that we have been following a delusion all along and that if we continue in this direction, our organization will become *nothing! Nothing at all!*"

I could see Dr. Scott becoming more and more agitated as I spoke, but I continued, making point after point, reading passages from the little book Dianne and I had spent the night reading and rereading. As I concluded my speech, I appealed to them to take some time to read *The Remnant Church* before making a decision. Then I sat down to await the board members' reactions.

Dr. Scott was the first to speak, although I could see that Bill Hughes was equally agitated. "Pastor John," he said, "You know that I respect you very much, and I'm willing to read the book. But frankly, I think you're getting a little too worked up over it. We've read these statements before. I've heard you preach sermons where you told people how to respond to others who might read these statements to them. Don't you think you're being a little hasty in saying we have to turn around one hundred and eighty degrees and go back to the General Conference? Think of all the things those people have done to us. Don't you remember the dirt they hurled at you in that *Issues* book?"

Doc hit a raw nerve when he brought that up, but somehow I couldn't even feel angry about that at the moment. The Lord had convicted me that I had been wrong in focusing on the sins of others; how could I get angry that others had treated me in the way that I had been treating them? We were all equally guilty and in need of a Saviour.

"I hear what you're saying, Doc," I responded. "All I'm doing is asking you to take the book and read it."

"But what about the camp meeting next week?" Bill Hughes asked. "You know what our plans are. Everyone is counting on us to bring Caleb and Joshua up to Pennsylvania to broadcast the call out of Babylon. You can't just back out on that at the last minute! People are counting on us!"

"I've thought of that, Bill," I responded. "I'm not saying we can't go up to Pennsylvania and take Caleb and Joshua to uplink the camp meeting. All I'm saying is that I'm not ready to join the others in proclaiming a call out of Babylon, and I'm not willing to allow our equipment to be used to deliver that message. I'm hoping you'll back me up on that."

Bill shook his head in dismay and frustration. "I don't know, Pastor John. This is all so contrary to what we've been saying—to the direction we've been going. I don't think it's fair to all of a sudden change your tune and expect everyone else to just come right along and sing harmony with you. I, for one, say we should go ahead as planned. If this new light you have is right, we can always backtrack."

"Are you kidding me, Bill?" I interrupted him. "How in the world do you think we can ever backtrack from a call to people to leave the organized church and join us? Once we issue that call, people will be committed. They will withdraw from their congregations. We can't ask them to do that unless we're absolutely positive that we're doing the right thing!"

The discussion shot back and forth across the table for some time, with the two men board members arguing passionately with me. Finally, in a lull, Patti spoke up in a quiet, almost quavering voice. "I've been sitting here listening to you men talk," she said. "And I deeply respect and love all of you. . . . I know the direction we've been going, and I've felt all along that it was right, but I have to admit that some things have been bothering me a lot lately. . . . I've been doing a lot of studying, reading, and praying on my own. I—well, I found some of the statements John has been reading to us—and some other ones, too, and I've really been praying that the Lord would lead us, because I couldn't feel comfortable speaking out against the church so strongly when I was reading those things." She paused before continuing. "I can't help but feel that the Lord has led you and Dianne to these same statements," she said. "I think we all need to study—to just put aside our personal opinions for a while and let the Lord lead us."

Doc and Bill had sat quietly while Patti spoke, but now they returned to their arguments for staying the course and considering things carefully before changing direction. Then Kathleen broke in with her first comments since I had spoken. I had noticed her watching Patti carefully as she spoke and had wondered what was going through her mind.

"Patti," Kathleen began, "I just want you to know that the Lord has been convicting me of many of the same things you mentioned. I just couldn't put some of the things I was reading about the church out of my mind, but I've always trusted Pastor John, and I couldn't believe that the Lord was leading him down the wrong path, so I just hadn't spoken up. But with what's been said here today, I can see it so clearly. The Lord has been leading all of us in the same direction, and He was just waiting for someone to be brave enough to speak up and share what they had learned." She looked at me then. "I'm very glad for what you've said today, Pastor John. I need to study this out a lot more, I know, but I agree that we can't go on following the path we have been on. We can't go ahead with the call to people to leave the organized church next week."

I looked at Doc and then at Bill. Both seemed perplexed, not sure which way to turn. They were clearly in the minority on the board, but they weren't at all convinced that the rest of us were right. By this time, Patti was in tears, wiping her eyes. Finally Doc spoke up. "I say we all get copies of *The Remnant Church* and read them for ourselves, then decide what to do."

"I agree," I responded. "But we've got to make one decision right away. Are we going to send Caleb and Joshua to Pennsylvania next week? I think we agree that we can't let them be used to broadcast the call out of the church. It's clear that the majority of the board supports me in that. I'm going to get on the phone to the other leaders and tell them that we won't be coming."

Speaking those words brought home a sense of the finality of the change of direction to me. Up to that point, I suppose I had still held onto the possibility that I was wrong and that the rest of the board could convince me to at least let the ministry go on in its own direction, even if I couldn't participate. Now I knew that the Lord had led me to my new position and that the board would back me up. Any thought of our ministry participating in any way in a call out of Babylon faded as I spoke those words.

CHAPTER 21

We closed that meeting with a long, heartfelt season of prayer, and then I walked quietly into my office, preparing myself for what I would say when I called the other ministry leaders. I was still sitting quietly at my desk when Bill and Doc came to the door. We discussed the issues further, and I insisted that I needed to inform the other ministries right away of our change of direction. But Doc and Bill had a better idea.

"Pastor John," Doc said, when I was ready to start making the calls. "We don't think it's best for you to call the other leaders. Why don't you let us make the calls?"

"No," I responded. "I'm the one under conviction here. I've led us this far into this situation, and it's my responsibility to finish what I've started."

"But wait," Bill said. "Doc and I have been talking about this. Just hear us out."

"Sure, Bill."

"If you call up one of the leaders and tell him what you just told us, how do you think he's going to respond?"

"Well, at first he'll probably start trying to reason with me. If that doesn't work, he'll no doubt start getting pretty frustrated, maybe even angry, and try to make me stand by our earlier commitment to come."

"That's right, and all you'll be able to do is argue with him and share your convictions. Then he'll share his, and where will it all end up? The two of you will still be in disagreement.

"But think of it this way," Bill continued. "What if I make the call? I can tell him that we've had just a bit of a setback here, and we're regrouping and studying and deciding which way we're going to go. Nothing's final yet. Pastor John's having some second thoughts, but Doc and I are still with you, and we'll just have to weather the storm for now—have a little patience until everything settles down. We're still working with Pastor John, trying to help him see that it's important to stay the course.

"Can't you see, Pastor, how much better that would be? It keeps the doors of communication open between us and the other ministries."

I had to agree with the two of them, and they were more than willing to make the phone calls. I stayed out of the conversations with the other ministry leaders, but Doc and Bill brought me regular reports. The calls didn't go well— there was a lot of frustration and anger that we were changing course so suddenly. We offered to bring the television equipment up to the camp meeting and to broadcast other parts of the meetings, but not the call out of Babylon or the message calling the organized Seventh-day Adventist Church Babylon. For taking this stand we were accused of exerting "kingly power" over them. The other leaders would not accept our offer. Either we had to broadcast 100 percent of the messages, or they would withdraw the invitation for us to attend.

And so it was decided that we would not participate in the camp meeting in Bethel, Pennsylvania, at all. When that news went out, the switchboard at Prophecy Countdown headquarters lit up like a Christmas tree. People from all over the country began calling in, asking questions, pleading with us to go ahead as planned. They looked to us as pillars of strength in the Historic Adventist Movement, and they accused us of crumbling under pressure and of backing down because of financial difficulties, but of course, none of that was true. We were simply moving according to the convictions the Lord had given to us, and as we did so, the true nature of the movement we had been a part of began to reveal itself as it never had before.

At first, people's reaction seemed to be one of confusion and dismay. They pled with us to reconsider. But when we didn't respond according to their wishes, many people's frustration turned to anger. The rumor mill began to churn out stories about us, and other ministries published scathing attacks on us, accusing us of turning back to the organized church purely for financial reasons. Those who believe such accusations can examine the records. If we changed directions for financial reasons, it was one of the most stupid things we could have done. Far from improving our financial situation, it actually led to the drying up of most of our income.

Within our own board, the division of opinions continued with Bill Hughes and Doctor Scott still not coming around. We all had been deeply wounded by the way the organized church had treated us, and we had accepted the arguments about that organization being Babylon. But some of us were now reconsidering that stand. Doc and Bill read the same material we did, but they could not accept that we had been wrong in our assessment.

I remained firm in my conviction that turning the ministry around had been the right thing to do, and as a result, the focus of my sermons changed.

Meanwhile, Doc and Bill encouraged me to keep on studying, to be sure that I wasn't missing something. Together we came up with the idea of inviting a variety of ministry leaders to come and meet with us to seriously study the question of whether or not the organized Seventh-day Adventist Church had become part of Babylon. Late in April we sent out invitations to a wide variety of independent ministries, inviting them to come to Orlando to meet with us for a weekend round-table discussion.

The kinds of responses we got shouldn't have surprised me. They wouldn't have surprised me if only I had always been able to see clearly the motivation that was the driving force behind the Historic Adventist Movement. While we all claimed we were motivated by love for the Lord and His last-day message, I have to admit now that there was an underlying thread of our need to run our own programs and not have to submit to any authority outside ourselves.

This spirit came through loud and clear in the responses we received from the invitees. Leader A declared that if we were not going to invite Leader B, then he wouldn't come. C said that if we were not going to invite D, we could count him out. The enmity between the various ministries was almost worse than their mutual enmity with the church. It seemed that everyone was pointing a finger at someone else.

Undaunted, we went ahead in faith, hoping that the Holy Spirit would overrule in these men's hearts and that at the last minute they would decide to come. We rented a retreat center and provided meals in anticipation of twenty or thirty guests. But to our dismay, only two people joined us. The center was set up with couches arranged in a square to accommodate a large number of participants. Now just five of us—three from Prophecy Countdown and two other leaders of independent ministries—sat together to study and pray.

We discussed the issues and prayed together, but with only three ministries represented, there wasn't much hope of making any progress. The one thing that did come clear to us, though, from our study, was that the Lord wants His people to be united. We read quotation after quotation about the importance of presenting a united front to the world. We focused our attention especially on the words found on page 311 of *The Desire of Ages*:

> Many are zealous in religious services, while between them and their brethren are unhappy differences which they might reconcile. God requires them to do all in their power to restore harmony. Until they do this, He cannot accept their services. The Christian's duty in this matter is clearly pointed out.

We realized that it was incumbent upon us to do everything in our power, by the grace of God, to bring about reconciliation among the various ministries.

The saying is that if the mountain won't come to Mohammed, then Mohammed will go to the mountain, and that's what we decided to do after that disastrous nonmeeting. Ron Woolsey, leader of the Narrow Way Ministry, was one of the two leaders who had come. He suggested that since the other leaders hadn't been willing to come and meet with us, we ought to find a way we could go and meet with them. Doc and I agreed with him that we should get involved in some sort of reconciliation ministry, to try to patch things up and bring the Historic Adventist Movement back into unity.

"I have a motor home," Doc said in one of our meetings. "Why don't the three of us make a trip together? We could visit all of the independent ministries and appeal to them to come together in harmony. Surely the Lord would bless us in an effort like that. It seems like we're all just talking past each other, calling names, and looking for things to criticize. Let's see if we can't do something to overcome this negative spirit. After all, isn't that what Jesus told us to do in Matthew 5? If our brother has anything against us, aren't we supposed to be the ones who go out and try to remedy the situation?"

I couldn't argue with his reasoning or with the generous offer of his motor home for the trip. Within a few days we loaded up the motor home and headed out on an 8,000-mile journey of reconciliation—at least we hoped that was what it would be.

CHAPTER

22

I n June of 1995 Bill Hughes, Dr. Al Scott, and I loaded our traveling
gear into Doc's 33-foot motor home and headed out to take our
appeal for unity and reconciliation to some of the most prominent independent ministries. The intent of this trip was not to call these other ministers
to reunite with the organized church. The three of us ourselves were not united
on the issue of whether the organized church was or was not Babylon. Even at
this time, neither Doc nor Bill had shifted his viewpoint a bit.

Rather, our goal was to meet with each of the ministry leaders and to
point out to them the importance of unity—to appeal to them to sit down
with us and work out our differences so that we could move ahead with a
strong, cooperative front. As it was, there was so much criticism and accusing going on between the various ministries, and so much competition for
funds, that our efforts were as futile as the builders' at Babel after the Lord
confused their tongues. In fact, with the multiplicity of messages going out
from all the major ministries, plus the error and fanaticism of all the little
spinoffs of those ministries, it appeared that "Historic Adventism" and the
whole independent ministry arena had become Babel, if not Babylon. It certainly had become confusion.

BACK ON TRACK

We plotted a course that would take us from the East Coast to the West Coast, starting in Virginia, working our way through the Midwest, then to California and from there up to Washington and Montana. Our itinerary would include Hartland (Colin Standish), then Behold the Lamb (Kenny Shelton) and Amazing Truth (Jan Marcussen) in Illinois. From there we would go to Kansas to meet with John Grosboll at Steps to Life. Next we would go to California to meet with Danny Vierra of Modern Manna. Then we would head north to Washington state to visit with Ron Spear of Hope International and then start east and stop in Troy, Montana, to meet with our friends at Printed Page Ministries. As things worked out, we followed a slightly different route but attempted to meet with all of these independent ministries.

Our first stop was at Hartland, after about a day on the road, and it was almost our last stop. When Prophecy Countdown first went independent back in 1985, Colin Standish, Ralph Larson, and Ron Spear had welcomed me with open arms, and we had produced a number of videotapes together. But the unity didn't last long. We are all highly independent thinkers with programs of our own. After a while, we realized that we couldn't work together—I think they saw me as being just too independent, and when they couldn't control me, they backed away. I hadn't had much interaction with Colin in recent years, but we were under strong conviction that we needed to try to bring about unity among the independent ministries, so we hoped and prayed for the best.

Our reception at Hartland was, at best, cool. Colin and a number of his associates met with us, but their attitude was somewhat skeptical. "Oh, you've gone back to the conference before, John," they said—implying that I was just waffling and that I would soon be changing my tune again.

We shared the passages we had been reading that had convicted us of the need to put aside our differences and work together to present a united front to the world, but our words seemed to be falling on deaf ears. "There will be unity," Standish said. "But only in the Holy Spirit's time." In other words, we didn't need to make any special efforts to unite. We would have to wait until the Spirit worked miraculously to bring about unity.

Our visit with the Hartland group was disheartening. If that was the kind of reaction we would meet at all our stops, the trip hardly seemed worthwhile. "This is a waste," I said when we were a few miles down the road.

"Let's just go back home." But the others weren't willing to give up so easily, so we headed for Illinois.

Kenny Shelton worked with his brother Danny in founding Three Angels Broadcasting in the early eighties, but around 1990 they had a falling out, and Kenny formed his own ministry called Behold the Lamb. Kenny had been at our Orlando meeting, and he welcomed us warmly and invited us to his Wednesday evening prayer meeting. We had a nice visit, but Kenny was, as usual, rather noncommittal when it came to forming a more united front.

Our next stop was to be at Amazing Truth Ministry. Located in rural Illinois, it proved challenging to find. By the time we finally noticed a tiny sign on a warehouse some distance from the road, we were about fifteen minutes late for our appointment with Jan Marcussen. Some of Jan's staff greeted us with the information that Jan had been up against a publication deadline for his newsletter and had left. They weren't sure when he would be back. They told us we were welcome to wait, but the atmosphere there seemed about like what we had found at Hartland. It appeared to us that Jan wasn't at all interested in what we might have to say.

We knew we were in the vicinity of the headquarters of Three Angels Broadcasting Network, but we hadn't planned on going there because this group had always stayed so tightly connected with the organized church. But under the circumstances I said, "Hey, we can't be treated any worse there than we have been already, so why not just stop by and see them?"

So we called Danny Shelton and asked if we could stop by. He said he would be happy to see us, so we drove on over. Much to our surprise, we received a very cordial welcome. Danny gave us a complete tour of the facilities. He was, of course, interested in unity, but his vision was broad enough to include the organized church as well, which most of the independent groups wouldn't consider.

Our next stop was to be in Kansas, so we were soon on the road again. We arrived in Wichita on Friday and phoned Steps to Life to let John Grosboll know we were there and that we would like to visit with him and his staff. John and I had been quite close in the early nineties, and I had looked to him as a sort of teacher. He is a deep thinker and a careful student. Even though he would never come right out and say that the General Conference had become part of Babylon, it was under his tutelage that many of the independent ministries had begun moving toward the idea that it was time to call Adventists out of the organized church. If only we could make some significant progress with John, it would make our whole trip worthwhile.

We had hoped to make our meeting here a sort of summit that might make up for the failure of the Orlando meeting. Ron Woolsey, leader of The Narrow Way, had assured us that he understood John Grosboll, and that John would be happy to meet with us. Ron planned to join us in Wichita. Kenny Shelton had also agreed to drive down to Wichita to join in the meeting. But when we phoned, John Grosboll had his office manager tell us that he wasn't interested in meeting with us.

I called Ron and reported the response we had gotten, and he decided that he wouldn't come either since there wasn't going to be a meeting. But about this time Kenny showed up and went out to Steps to Life and said that he had driven for eight hours and he wasn't going to leave without something happening. Finally John Grosboll agreed to allow us to come to his church services on Sabbath, but he wouldn't agree to meet with us.

The church services at Steps to Life are usually videotaped for distribution, and I had understood that the services this week were to be taped. But that plan must have changed when our group showed up for church. We attended the Prairie Meadows Church at Steps to Life Sabbath morning, and finally at the end of the day the leaders agreed to meet with us.

The meeting did not start off well. There seemed to be very little interest in making a sincere effort to put aside differences and strive for unity. One of the first things to come up was a series of accusations against Prophecy Countdown—questions about our sincerity and the way that we handled our personnel.

What happened at this meeting clearly illustrates one of the major problems that the independent ministries face. To begin with, their staffs are often made up of people who do not respond well to authority or hierarchical structure. Whenever there is an authority problem or a disciplinary problem within a ministry, the measures taken are limited to that ministry. All too often when a person is disciplined in one ministry, he or she simply goes and joins up with another ministry with no accounting for what happened in the past.

Oftentimes these people, who have had a falling-out at one ministry, go as talebearers to a new place and use the new ministry as a weapon to try to justify themselves or to avenge what they believe was mistreatment. Several people at Steps to Life now took the side of individuals who had resigned over the San Bernardino issue or been disciplined at Prophecy Countdown and challenged our right to discipline them. Others made accusations against Bill Hughes, who at that time was separated from his wife, saying that he shouldn't be out here trying to reconcile with others if he couldn't even reconcile with his wife.

We discussed these issues back and forth, without much success. But after the initial coldness, we managed to work our way around to some more constructive topics, and the Steps to Life leaders agreed that we ought to strive for unity—especially when it came to the issues surrounding the short-wave radio ministry. After the rather discouraging start, we came to agree that there were at least some areas that we ought to try to work together on. Being the eternal optimist, I left the meeting feeling very good about the possibilities of bringing a new unity to the Historic Adventist Movement. Doc and Bill were also encouraged.

We had planned to go from Wichita to California but for some reason decided to change course and go up to Troy, Montana, first, to visit Printed Page Ministries. There the Lord had another lesson for us to learn, but it wasn't evident at first.

We arrived in Troy in the midst of a major crisis at Printed Page. A prominent leader there had just admitted to being involved in improper activity, and other staff members sought our counsel as to how to proceed. The leader seemed repentant, and the staff asked the three of us to meet with them to recommend some action. The leader agreed to accept whatever decision our group came to.

We sensed the Lord's leading in this. After changing our planned itinerary, we arrived at just the time when we were needed. While we were distressed to see a man who had worked with us having problems, we were glad that we were there at the right time to minister discipline in a redemptive fashion. At the board's invitation, we met with two board members and agreed on what seemed a reasonable disciplinary course. The leader was to move off the campus and step completely out of ministry for six months and then the situation would be reevaluated. As promised, he agreed to abide by our recommendation.

We left Troy saddened but encouraged as well, for it seemed that here, at least, was one ministry where some accountability to proper church discipline was being observed. The leader had made himself accountable to other servants of God, not just to those within his own group.

Unfortunately, we were soon proven wrong. Although the leader agreed to step down from his position, he never moved off the campus and never relinquished the control he exercised over finances. The Printed Page board never followed through with an official action removing him, and within two weeks the leader had reneged on everything he had agreed to do and had begun to spread the story that John Osborne had come to his ministry and tried to take away his power.

Looking back on that experience, it seems to me that the Lord was working very hard to point out to me the problems that plagued the independent ministries. With no accountability outside the local organization, a strong leader can just about get away with murder, and anyone who doesn't agree with the decision of one group can easily move on to another group. As long as that is the case, and as long as ministries are led by people who refuse to recognize any authority but their own, there will never be true unity among the independent ministries. The Historic Adventist Movement may be united on a few doctrinal points, but there is such intense individualism, and at times competition among the various ministries, that they can no more unite for the finishing of God's work than the builders of Babel could unite to finish their tower.

From Montana we went to Eatonville, Washington, to meet with the board of Hope International. We had a cordial meeting there. Several of the board members were very supportive of Prophecy Countdown, but once again we came up against the basic principle of independent ministries. Their independence is more important than unity. We sensed no hostility at Hope International, but neither did we feel that we had accomplished anything as far as establishing a more united movement. The rest of our trip was equally fruitless.

Danny Vierra, of Modern Manna, had been a frequent health speaker at Prophecy Countdown's camp meetings. He was holding a camp meeting of his own when we arrived in California, and I called and asked if we could come see him. Another independent ministry leader had called and warned him that I was on my way and told him not to receive me. When he refused to let me come, Doc got on the phone and asked if *he* could attend the meetings, but Danny responded simply that if Doc came, Danny would have to explain why he was there, and he didn't want to have to do that.

By now we were thoroughly discouraged. We had felt that the Lord had led us to make this trip in order to bring a message of reconciliation and unity to His scattered flock. But we had been rebuffed at almost every turn. It was clear to us that Colin Standish's observation had been correct. True unity will only come on the Holy Spirit's timetable. We felt convicted that we had to do everything in our power to overcome the things that divided us, but it didn't seem that any of the other ministry leaders were tuned in to the same message. Each was content to go his own way, unimpeded by the opinions or the messages others might be receiving from the Lord.

After the motor-home trip, we returned to Mount Dora in the middle of June. Bill Hughes made some personal marital decisions which affected his ability to continue as a loyal member of the Prophecy Countdown Board and the principal of the school. These decisions eventually led to his separation from our organization in August 1995.

Labor Day weekend 1995, Doc attended a camp meeting sponsored by Thomas Jackson, a health educator in Tennessee. Jackson heads an independent health ministry that works with, and in support of, the organized work of God's church.

One of the speakers at the meeting was a physician from Texas. Nobody can get to a physician like a fellow physician. This doctor presented a series of talks on how to relate to God's church, using the biblical examples of Moses, Elijah, and Christ. The Holy Spirit used that series of talks to speak to Doc's heart. He came home a changed man. All of his bitterness had just evaporated into thin air as he came to terms with what had happened to him in Arizona. He became able to forgive those who had wronged him in the name of God and the Seventh-day Adventist Church.

When Doc returned to Prophecy Countdown, he reviewed communications from former employees and supporters who fanatically believed that the Seventh-day Adventist Church organization was the Babylon of Revelation 18. These communications were so filled with hate, recriminations, accusations, and criticism that Doc did a complete restudy of the "Babylon issue." He found an article by Ellen G. White, published in the *Review and Herald*, November 8, 1956, that summarized the material very well. (This article also appears in volume six of the bound *Review and Herald* articles.) One morning Doc excitedly came to my office and outlined the following:

First, the message that identifies the organized Seventh-day Adventist Church with Babylon and that calls people to come out of it is of satanic origin. It is a spurious and erroneous message. Second, the messengers giving this message are "misled," have placed their own false construction on the *Testimonies*, are "working on the enemy's side, not on God's side," are under "the inspiration of satanic agencies," are not "working in Christ's lines," are "listening to the voice of a stranger," have placed themselves in a position where Satan casts "his hellish shadow athwart their pathway to obstruct every ray of light," are "grievous wolves," "speaking perverse things," are in Satan's service, have "stood by the side of the accuser of the brethren," are "on the wrong track," are "helping Satan to cast upon the kingdom of Christ reproach," have slipped unconsciously into work in Satan's lines "without perceiving that [they] have changed leaders," and are helping Satan by "denouncing, accusing, and condemning." Thus a person who truly desires to know the truth and to be set free from satanic delusions can, by a humble and repentant spirit, return to God's historic truths.

Wow, had my associate pastor ever changed! We were now together on the same road. We cried, prayed, and praised God together! We knew things were going to get a lot rougher before they got better—but we would face them together.

CHAPTER 23

After our failed attempts at unity, I began preaching a series of sermons entitled "The Elijah Message to Laodicea." In these I began expounding my new understanding of the nature of the church, trying to lead those who had followed me in rebellion against the church to turn back toward the organization with me. I suppose I was a bit unclear in the direction I was heading at that time, because I wasn't really ready to reunite with the organized church myself. There were still a lot of issues to be resolved in my mind. The seed of bitterness was still bearing its fruit, and I couldn't picture myself reconciling with those whom I felt had treated me badly.

As I continued to preach my new message, it soon became evident that if Prophecy Countdown was no longer going to be a central clearinghouse for criticism of church leadership, many supporters whom we had thought were loyal to us would find others to champion their cause.

Finances had been tight for some time. We had planned to raise the full $5.5 million to purchase the WVHA shortwave station in six months' time. That all fell apart at San Bernardino in February 1994, so much of the rest of that year was spent in fund-raising and finally making arrangements to borrow $3.5 million to complete the purchase. We believed that once the station was secure, people would resume their support. The climate had been very shaky and people were withholding their money to see what would happen. But instead, as more and more people began to recognize that we had made a full turnabout and that we never again would be proclaiming messages highly critical of the organized Adventist Church, contributions continued to shrink. Soon we were in a basic struggle just to survive. We had to cut back broadcasts from WVHA, and soon we were releasing staff members at our headquarters.

Reports continued to pour in of people who had been led to the Lord through the positive aspects of our television and radio ministries, and we publicized these results to those on our donor lists. Our efforts brought in some continuing support, but nowhere near the $250,000 per month that had been the basis for our budget at the height of our success as an independent ministry focusing on the sins of the church.

One by one, we were forced to close down aspects of our ministry. In 1993 we had moved into a 24,000 square-foot office complex. We had also branched out into a health-food ministry and opened a small vegetarian restaurant. We were in the midst of a construction project, turning an unused section of our office building into a new and improved television studio. We had our own twelve-grade academy, and our seven-hundred-member church had a staff of five. All together, the ministry had fifty-five employees.

Soon we could no longer afford to operate our twelve-grade school. With attendance dwindling, we relinquished the lease for our church sanctuary and moved our services into a studio in our office building. We kept the health-food ministry and vegetarian restaurant open for some time, but as cash flow tightened, even these businesses that brought in some funds had to be sacrificed.

Our diminished cash flow was further eroded when other independent ministries continued printing false accusations against us in order to further undermine our support base. This type of behavior had been going on since the split at San Bernardino, but it had really intensified in the past year because of the theological position we took regarding God's church.

Our ministry had a faithful payment history with those who had invested their means with us. This can be substantiated through our audited financial statements. But when cash flow diminishes, the obvious result is an inability to meet financial obligations. And this was where we found ourselves in November 1996.

As a result, people have tried to stir up matters in the local media, and this has served to weaken our ability to repay debts even further. After one local T.V. station stirred up a media blitz to increase their viewership during ratings sweeps-week, a request for information was made by the State of Florida. But even after close to a year of scrutiny no action has ever been instituted against Prophecy Countdown. There has been absolutely nothing tangible, no improprieties of any type, to justify the media frenzy that was stirred up by disgruntled "Historic Adventists."

I had recognized in April of 1995, when I first accepted the fact that things had to change, that we stood to lose everything that we had built up through the years. Still, it was difficult and painful to watch it all disintegrating right in front of our eyes. We would reflect back over the global outreach of our ministry during the past seventeen years and think of the hundreds and hundreds of people who were, in fact, baptized into the Seventh-day Adventist Church from the evangelistic outreach of our ministry. Many nights Dianne and I stayed up late, praying and seeking to know God's intention for us. But it seemed that there was no light at the end of the tunnel. The further we went in the direction we sensed the Lord leading, the darker it got. Our only hope was in His promise that He would not lead us otherwise than we would choose to be led if we could see the end from the beginning.

Though we were trying to follow the Lord's leading, we couldn't see a clear path before our feet. We knew that we couldn't continue to condemn the organized church. But on the other hand, so much dirty water had gone under the bridge between us and the church that we didn't see how we could possibly go back. What sort of response would we get from leadership? They had every right to be suspicious of us, since we had reconciled with them once before in 1987 and by 1990 had gone back to being critical.

During all the years of our criticizing the conference, my brother David, who is the senior pastor of the Carmichael Seventh-day Adventist Church in Sacramento, had watched and prayed, hoping that something would turn me around. Although I had lived with him while attending La Sierra College, we had never developed a real brotherly closeness. He is eleven years older than I am, so we hadn't been particularly close at home either. Nevertheless, David was to play a major role in helping us to find the direction the Lord was trying to lead us.

In August of 1996, there was a big Osborne family reunion in Florida, after my nephew, Chad Kirstein, was married in Avon Park. My mother's brother, Art Felice, who works closely with the church administration in southern California, approached me first. Then, so did my brother David. Neither of them knew of the other's burden. In a very frank and open way, each told me privately that he thought I ought to be doing more to reconcile myself with the organized church.

"No way," I responded. "There's just no way they're even interested in hearing from me. Not after all the things I've said and done. I've gone too far to try to come back now."

Both allowed me to have my opinion, but our extended family had reserved two villas on the beach for an entire week, so David kept coming back to me, telling me that he thought that what he and Uncle Art had stated earlier, that the church had changed in the years since I had left was true. "The brethren have learned some lessons in dealing with independent ministries," he assured me. "The church is bigger, broader-minded now. They've learned that heavy-handed tactics don't work. There's room for people like you today."

I wasn't sure if what they were saying was right. It sounded too good to be true, and I still had reservations about coming back to the church. For years I had focused on the bad aspects of the church, and certainly the organization has made some wrong decisions. But, on the other hand, I had been under strong conviction about the importance of unity. While these men were pressing their point with me, that statement from *The Desire of Ages*, page 311, seemed to jump out at me again and hit me squarely in the forehead:

> Many are zealous in religious services, while between them and their brethren are unhappy differences which they might reconcile. God requires them to do all in their power to restore harmony. Until they do this, He cannot accept their services. The Christian's duty in this matter is clearly pointed out.

Suddenly I realized that if the conference leaders were not a part of Babylon, then they were my *brethren!* If the Lord was going to continue to accept my service in any way, I needed to do all that I could to restore harmony with *them*, just as I had tried to do with the independent ministries on numerous occasions. Finally I agreed that if someone in conference administration were willing, I would at least consent to enter into dialogue.

Within a few days, David had contacted the Florida Conference president, Elder Obed Graham. Elder Graham had been in conference administration for nearly twenty years. He had been present at many of the meetings where I had interacted with the conference, and had been a participant in the decisions the conference made about me, including disfellowshiping me and disbanding our church. For several years at the beginning of our ministry, he had also served on the board of Prophecy Countdown. Elder Graham sent back word through David that he would be willing to meet with me.

It wasn't an easy thing to set up such a meeting. I wasn't willing to go to the conference office, and conference leaders wouldn't have felt comfortable coming to our offices either. So we rented a meeting room at Embassy Suites in Altamonte Springs, Florida.

I could sense a lot of tension around Prophecy Countdown as we prepared for that meeting. And a lot of the tension was in my own heart. I still harbored hard feelings about the way I had been treated by the conference, and I wasn't going to let those issues just fall by the wayside. In order to be sure that we got a fair hearing and that there would be a fair reporting of what happened, I took four members of our board, including Dianne, with me. The conference was represented by Elder Graham and Elder Lewis Hendershot, the conference vice president. My brother David was there as the mediator. Even he admitted, in talking with us before the meeting, that there was a good chance that there would be blood on the walls—figuratively speaking—at the end of that meeting. He knew how strong the feelings were, and he didn't anticipate that everything could be resolved in one meeting.

I went into that meeting, in September of 1996, with grave concerns, having no idea what to expect. As I talked with our board before the meeting, I told them that I didn't see how very positive results could come out of the meeting, because we all had a history of five years of hate and resentment and anger and hostility. The meeting might end up being nothing more than a time to vent old hostilities. But we could at least hope to get something started, and perhaps in a second or third meeting we would be able to make some meaningful progress.

Elder Graham, Elder Hendershot, and David all met us in the lobby. We shook hands in greeting and then went to our meeting room. David, as mediator, sat at the head of the table. "Let's begin this meeting with prayer," he said after the initial greetings were over.

We all knelt around the table. I must admit that I didn't hear a lot of the prayer. My mind was busy rehearsing the plans we had. We had brought files with us—evidence we could use in our defense and evidence of the wrongs we felt had been done. We were ready to answer whatever accusations the brethren might have against us, and we were ready with our own salvos to fire back at them.

As we rose from our knees and took our seats, David said a few words about why we were meeting then looked at Elder Graham. "Elder Graham, I'd like to give you the opportunity to speak first," he said. "I understand that you have something that you would like to say to John."

"Yes I do," Elder Graham said. He was seated almost directly across the table from me, and now he looked me straight in the eye. "John, we've had a lot of association together through the years. Some of it good, and some of it not so good," he began. "And I would just like to open this meeting by telling you that I know that the conference has made some mistakes in dealing with you, and that I'm sorry for it." He paused and looked down the row at each member of my board then looked straight at me again.

"John," he continued. "I want to apologize and ask your forgiveness, especially for the way that things were handled when you were disfellowshiped from the conference church back in 1991. You and I had worked out an agreement as to how your membership was to be handled, but when I went into the committee meeting, things changed rather rapidly, and it ended up with your being summarily disfellowshiped without a right to appeal. It wasn't supposed to be that way, and I am sorry that that was the outcome. You were not treated right, and it was my fault for not doing everything I could to stop that action from being taken."

I could hear Elder Graham speaking, but I could hardly believe my ears. I was almost in shock to hear this man, who had done so much in the years since 1990 to discredit my ministry, apologizing, asking my forgiveness, and admitting that he and his committee had been wrong in the way they had handled my membership.

I still had some fight in me though. It was one thing for him to say this in a closed meeting, but would he publicly apologize for what had been done?

I challenged him with that question, and he told me, before all those witnesses, that he was willing to do whatever I wanted. He would even come to our ministry and speak live over our satellite network, saying the same things he had just said.

I felt a lump coming into my throat. How could I do anything but accept his apology and forgive him? There were tears in my eyes and a shake in my voice as I responded, thanking him for his forthrightness and in turn apologizing and asking forgiveness for some of the things that Prophecy Countdown had done that had wounded Elder Graham and the Florida Conference.

Never in our wildest dreams had we anticipated that the meeting would go the way it did. The tone of the meeting was set by that opening statement, and the results were totally opposite from what I had feared they might be. It opened up a little light at the end of the tunnel for Dianne and me. We had been journeying in darkness long enough, and now we could see that there was hope at the end—that perhaps, despite all that we had done to wound God's church, perhaps we could be accepted back into fellowship, back into the light of God's organized, remnant church that He wants to lead right through the last days and into His kingdom.

CHAPTER 24

A fter that first meeting in early September 1996, we stayed in close contact with Elder Graham, and he became a sort of pastoral counselor to us. As our relationship strengthened, I came to realize that it was time to fish or cut bait. I had been leading our supporters and home churches away from the precipice for a year and a half. It was now time to call everyone to make a decision. I hoped that we could bring our followers back into harmony with the organized Seventh-day Adventist Church.

After establishing a dialogue with the Florida Conference officials, we were providentially blessed as Elder Bill May came upon the scene. Elder May had been a conference leader for years and was one of the original founders of the Amazing Facts ministry. He had actually called Elder Joe Crews into that ministry. Elder May now lived in the Orlando area.

The Prophecy Countdown Board had reached the consensus that God wanted it to establish a supportive relationship with the conference church. The board met with Elder May and with much prayer mapped out a plan to bring speakers to Prophecy Countdown and the Rolling Hills church to help with the transition. The speakers had to be men who were sound in their biblical interpretation, solid in their understanding that Ellen G. White was, and is, God's last-day prophet to His remnant church, and supportive of God's denominated Seventh-day Adventist Church.

Many names were discussed. During this time, Patti Edwards, our treasurer and a Prophecy Countdown board member, had gone to visit friends in North Carolina. There she obtained tapes of a recent series held by Willard Santee. These messages addressed in a powerful way the conflict between the organized work and the independent work.

We made contact with Elder Santee, and while he was supportive of our position, he did not have the time or the authority to come to Florida, particularly to an independent church such as Rolling Hills.

So I went to Elder Graham one day and told him that I had decided that we needed to bring a speaker to Prophecy Countdown who would be accepted both by the home church group and by the conference. I wanted someone to come who could deal plainly with the issues of the church and independent ministries.

As we discussed this possibility, I suggested the name of Willard Santee. Willard had gone through some very rough times himself. He had been a pastor; a situation had been handled badly, and he had been dismissed. He had become bitter and left the church to form his own independent group. He had come very close to calling the organized church Babylon. But since that time he had repented, returned, and now was serving as a conference pastor in Oregon.

Elder Graham agreed to make the contact with the Oregon Conference, and a few days later Willard called me on the phone. His president had told him that we wanted him to come to Prophecy Countdown for a camp meeting to preach a series of five sermons in a weekend series to be broadcast live over both shortwave radio and our satellite television network. He sounded thrilled with the opportunity, so we quickly made plans and established the weekend of November 16, my forty-fifth birthday, as the date. He would start on Friday evening, the fifteenth, with one sermon; then on Sabbath he would lead out in Sabbath School, preach the sermon for church, then hold another meeting at 2:00 p. m., and a final meeting beginning at 4:00 p. m.

That may sound like a pretty heavy schedule for a speaker, if you've mainly attended conference camp meetings where speakers usually have only one or two engagements in a day, but it's standard operating procedure for the independent ministries. When we invite a guest speaker to one of our meetings, they often speak four or five times on a Sabbath.

We sent out thousands of invitations to this special series, to supporters and others around our area. And I made contact with other independent ministry leaders, asking them to come and be a part of this weekend series. I went into the weekend with great hopes and expectations, praying that the Lord would bring hundreds to our meetings and especially hoping that the other leaders would be there and that Elder Santee's presentations would help them to come to the same position that Prophecy Countdown had come to—to be a supportive ministry of God's organized church.

We set up a large tent in the Prophecy Countdown parking lot. Only about eighty people showed up for the first meeting on Friday night. Of all the other ministry leaders I had invited, only Ron Woolsey and his wife, Claudia, came. Attendance held at about that level throughout the series. There is no way for us to know how many were tuned in via satellite television in the U. S. and via shortwave in Europe and Africa.

Elder Santee preached a powerful series in which he repeatedly called us to consider the meaning of the song of Moses and the Lamb. He spoke of Moses' experience in pleading for the people of Israel when God had declared that He was going to destroy them and raise up a new nation from Moses' seed. At that time Moses pled with God to forgive and spare the people. In the same way, Jesus, on Mt. Calvary, pled with God to forgive those who were crucifying Him, for they knew not what they were doing. Elder Santee appealed for us to learn to sing this song, which pleads with God to save His wayward children, instead of spending our time crying aloud and declaring the sins of the church before the world.

Elder Santee also dealt with many passages from the Bible and Ellen White's writings, as well as items from recent newspaper articles, all pointing to the fact that the final movements before the Second Coming are taking place right now. And he emphasized repeatedly, reading extensive passages from the Spirit of Prophecy, that God *never* predicted a time when people would be called out of the organized Seventh-day Adventist Church.

One illustration I found particularly compelling was a diagram of the church as two superimposed circles. Elder Santee illustrated how there are people in the church who pull to the right, while others pull to the left, and the two circles start moving in opposite directions. But there is still a group in the overlapping area—in the center. And the harder the two groups pull, the tighter they compact that group in the center, pulling them together in tighter and tighter unity.

Next, he shared a quotation from the Spirit of Prophecy predicting that those who pull in either direction, either toward fanaticism or toward unbelief, will finally come into harmony with each other in opposition to those in the middle, who remain faithful to God (see *Review and Herald*, 6 June, 1878). He added to that a story about his own experience of meeting with a prominent leader of an independent group who said simply that "the one thing that unites all of us [independents] is our hatred of the organized church."

It was now plain to all present where Elder Santee stood. Unfortunately, as he made some of his stronger points, individuals, and sometimes whole families, would stand up and walk out of the tent, never to return.

He shared passages such as this one from an article in the August 29, 1893, issue of the *Review and Herald*:

> When any one arises, either among us or outside of us, who is burdened with a message which declares that the people of God are numbered with Babylon, and claims that the loud cry is a call to come out of her, you may know that he is not bearing the message of truth. Receive him not, nor bid him God-speed; for God has not spoken by him, neither has he given a message to him, but he has run before he was sent.

On Sabbath morning, during the church service, Elder Santee departed from his planned sermon and simply shared with us, tearfully at times, the story of his own life—of his longing for God and righteousness, of his quest for peace and joy, and of how his zeal for doing right had finally led him into conflict with "the brethren" and had led to his expulsion from the ministry.

He spoke of the various groups he had associated with through the years, using the term "holy huddles" to describe the sense of elitism that too often abides among those who separate themselves from the church. Then he told us of how a seasoned pastor, Elder Stanley Folkenberg, who has a son named Bob, had finally come and ministered the true love of God to him and brought him the peace and joy he had longed for.

By the time Elder Santee launched into his final sermon at four o'clock on Sabbath afternoon, I knew that it was time for him to call us all to make a decision about our relationship to the Seventh-day Adventist Church. He began by telling us that we stand at a crossroads—that now is the time to make a decision about which way we will go.

Taking 2 Thessalonians 2:1-4 as his text, he reminded us that the Lord will not come until there has been a falling away—a great shaking and apostasy among God's people. "But," he said. "Those who are shaken out do *not* constitute the remnant." He knew the rationalizations that we had used. He had used them himself at one time. But now we could see that here was a deeply spiritual man, under strong conviction, and that he had come to realize that he had been wrong when he had taken the attitude that people needed to be called out of the church into a new remnant.

It was indeed decision time, and as Elder Santee reviewed the way that God had led His people in the past and the guidance that He had sent through the woman he referred to affectionately as simply "Ellen," he kept reminding us that it was time for us to make a decision as to how we would respond to the call to be a part of God's true remnant church.

As he moved toward the call that I knew was coming, he reviewed his own experience and how one pastor had been willing to accept him back into the church. "Because we were willing to work together, God allowed healing to take place. And beloved, if it happened to me, a chief of the rebels, it can certainly happen to any of you. God is longing for His people to come home.

"God is giving a last warning call to this church, and to those who are fighting this church, both inside and out, that it's time for *us* to come together in unity. Today I want to give you an opportunity . . . You're not responding to me; you're responding to God.

"God and all of heaven is interested in this very study . . . They are waiting with baited breath, as it were, to see *who* is going to activate his or her choice."

As for me, I knew already that I would be one of those who would take action in favor of the church, and I lifted my heart in earnest prayer, pleading for the souls of those around me, asking God's Holy Spirit to minister in a powerful way and appeal to their hearts to leave behind the anger and bitterness that had separated them from His remnant people.

"Who is going to be the first to come forward," Elder Santee continued. "Who is going to be the first to say 'God, remember me in your kingdom. I want to come back. I want to be an active part of your last-day call to the world to come out of Babylon. I don't want to be in Babylon; I want to be out of Babylon. And even though I'm in captivity, I want to be captured more by Jesus.' "

As he continued his appeal, he asked how many simply wanted to make a commitment to be a part of God's kingdom. He reminded us that many of us had done things that had deeply offended the leaders of the church and that we couldn't go back and smugly expect to be received with open arms. "I had to *earn* the respect of the brethren," he said. He reminded us that just as Saul, who persecuted the church of God, had to go out in the desert and find a personal relationship with God and be humbled, so we would need to discover that it is in our weakness that we will find true strength.

"Who, having heard God speak to your heart today, would like to respond and say, 'God I don't know what this means. I don't know when I might be able to join your church . . . but I would like to be able to come back. I'd like to be a part of that last message that's given to the world.'

"If you'd like to do that, will you just come and join me right down here in the front, today? I challenge you to do it. I know it takes a lot of courage."

I knew what I had to do. Humbly, and shaking with excitement, I stood to my feet. I wasn't the first to the front. My heart leapt with joy when I saw that my dear friend and associate Doctor Scott had beaten me. Soon Dianne was standing as well, making her way down the aisle. Silently I poured out my heart to the Lord, appealing to Him, asking that His holy angels and the Holy Spirit would be in this place, moving on hearts and drawing each soul who was listening, anywhere in the world, to Him.

One by one, others in the congregation began to stand and to move toward the front. I opened my eyes and looked around me. Kathleen Greenfield, our board chairman, was standing nearby and so was Patti Edwards, our treasurer. Our board stood united in our dedication to return and become a part of God's remnant church once again.

About twenty members of the Rolling Hills congregation also came forward. Another thirty or forty stayed in their seats, stone faced, not responding to the call. It hurt me deeply to see that so many were still not ready, after all I had done to try to lead them back. In a state of alarm, I went to the microphone and said some things that I thought would strengthen the appeal, but the depth of my concern came out more harshly than I wanted it to. Suddenly I remembered that this time I was the one responding to the call, not giving it. So I left the podium and took my position as one simply coming forward in response to Elder Santee's call.

When the meeting closed, some of those who had not responded came up to me. Still filled with hatred and anger at the church, they denounced me loudly as a false shepherd. But at the same time others were coming up and hugging Dianne and me, speaking praises to the Lord that we had had the courage to turn around and lead the way back to the church.

There were people in the parking lot until late that night. Some arguing, others praying, others singing the praises of the Lord. One particularly bright spot for me was the response of Ron and Claudia Woolsey. They had been leading out in an independent ministry for several years, and now they came forward and took their stand.

As for me, none of the turmoil around me could quiet the song in my heart. None of the criticisms, complaints, accusations, or recriminations that were hurled at me by those who were still angry, bitter, and hateful could dampen my spirit, for I knew that at last I was on my way home again.

There would be hard times to follow, especially when the magnitude of what I had done in leading others out of God's church weighed upon me. But I have come to realize that these individuals must make their own choices. I was glad to have my toes pointed in the right direction and that I had done what I could to try to bring them home with me.

Epilogue

After the November camp meeting, our church dwindled to about eighty members. The others left, and we haven't heard from most of them since. But I was gladdened by news that Ron and Claudia Woolsey had been accepted back into conference ministry and that they had been able to bring their two congregations with them. They had also been involved in ministry in Romania, and when they made a trip to that country, their followers there also reunited with the church.

The Rolling Hills congregation continued to meet in the television studio at Prophecy Countdown headquarters, and we continued to broadcast our church services live for several months. During this time we put forth Herculean efforts to find a way to continue funding our evangelistic outreach through the WVHA shortwave station. We cut back on the power of the signal, while we continued cutting staff and cutting broadcast time. Our task became increasingly difficult as we continued to receive salvos of criticism from certain independent ministries—berating us and twisting our position toward reconciliation and even criticizing the sermons that Willard Santee presented. They proclaimed to the world that our ministry had collapsed, without ever once calling us to find out the real situation.

BACK ON TRACK

In March of 1997, we sent out a special issue of our newsletter, fully explaining the reason for our new position and describing the wonderful results of our shortwave ministry (see Appendix). Support increased slightly, but we still couldn't afford to maintain that ministry. Finally, several months later, we worked out a deal with the organization that had financed the purchase, and it took over ownership of the station.

The criticism we were receiving from a number of independent ministries, and the negative publications they produced, resulted in confusion among our support base. During the month of May, our donations plummeted to the point that we had to cut our staff to the bare bones. We could no longer sustain the Rolling Hills Church, and May 24 was the last Sabbath for services there. It was an emotional time for us as we closed out that phase of our ministry.

On May 31 Dianne, Wesley, and I attended the Florida Conference camp meeting at Forest Lake Academy. We entered the auditorium with fear and trepidation, wondering what sort of response we would get when people recognized us. We spotted some empty chairs near the back of the auditorium and tried to make our entry as unobtrusive as possible. But soon people spotted us and began coming up to us and greeting us. Every one of them smiled warmly and gave us a heartfelt Christian welcome to camp meeting.

We were home at last. It was the best feeling I had known in many years.

But a better day was still to come. The next Sabbath we began attending a little church about an hour's drive from our home. The Clermont Seventh-day Adventist Church is pastored by an old friend of mine from Tennessee, Elder Jim King. He and his congregation welcomed us with open arms. I soon made a special request of that little church, and on Sabbath, July 12, I was rebaptized into God's remnant church. My heart nearly exploded with joy at the way God's church welcomed me back after so many years when I had done everything in my power to wound it. I was truly humbled, and excited at the same time, at the possibilities that lay before me now, for working together with this small church in continuing to spread the three angels' messages in preparation for the return of Jesus.

As I look at how I have lived my life, and how God has worked with me, I identify so much with the apostle Peter—both before and after his moment of truth in Pilate's judgment hall. Chapter 85 of *The Desire of Ages* has become precious to me. It is so encouraging that I have read it over and over again during this past year.

People often ask me how I relate to the church now that I am back, and I respond by telling a little story. A few years ago I had the opportunity to visit Russia to hold some meetings there. It was a great experience. I appreciated the opportunity a lot and enjoyed my time in Russia.

But when my plane landed at John F. Kennedy Airport in New York and I disembarked and set foot on American soil once again, I broke into spontaneous song. Other passengers and total strangers smiled, and some gave me a thumbs-up sign as I strode down the concourse, singing, "God Bless America!"

I know that my country isn't perfect. I know that wrong things are done here. But I've traveled to many other countries on this planet, and whenever I return to America, I'm just glad to be home. I've been all over the world, and there's nothing better out there!

That's the way I feel about my church as well. I've been on the outside, and believe me, there's nothing better out there. God raised up the Seventh-day Adventist Church to be His messenger to the world in these final days of history. It's God's seventh, last, and only church. It isn't perfect. But there's nothing better out there.

I was tempted to load up this book with inspired texts and quotes, but I've refrained from doing so. But I've just got to close with one quotation:

> Has God no living church? He has a church, but it is the church militant, not the church triumphant. We are sorry that there are defective members, that there are tares amid the wheat. . . . Although there are evils existing in the church, and will be until the end of the world, the church in these last days is to be the light of the world that is polluted and demoralized by sin. The church, enfeebled and defective, needing to be reproved, warned, and counseled, is the only object upon earth upon which Christ bestows His supreme regard (*Testimonies to Ministers*, 45, 49).

What more is there to say except—God bless the Seventh-day Adventist Church! Praise God, I'm home at last!

Appendix

In March of 1997, Prophecy Countdown sent out a newsletter explaining our change of course in relation to the organized church. What follows is excerpted from the text of that newsletter:

March, 1997

Dear Adventist Friend:

Events of recent months at Prophecy Countdown have brought the light of truth to our ministry concerning God's organized Church, and a powerful reformation in all our lives. We have had a growing conviction that we needed to seek unity and resolve the unhappy differences that we have had in past years with the Conference brethren, as much as it was in our power to do so. . . .

Inspiration makes clear that ministers have a responsibility laid upon us by God, to sometimes present very strong messages. But we must have "tears of love" in our voices when we do, just as Jesus did when He uttered His most scathing rebukes. And folks, I must confess, that those "tears of love" have not always been in my voice when I preached, and for that—I have asked God, and I now ask you (and all those I have needlessly hurt), for forgiveness!

Friend, you must agree, our Christian experience and walk with the Lord must be constantly growing and becoming more like Jesus. And for us to be more like Jesus, we need to follow His example, and get involved in the SOLUTION to the overwhelming problems that are flooding in upon God's people—and not pass by with self-righteous indignation, and "give up" on God's remnant Church! (As I once did!)

I believe that it is God's plan for the faithful laity, ministers, and ministries, both in the organized and self-supporting work, to JOIN HANDS to finish the work. Our journey to the kingdom is nearing its end, and what we do for the salvation of others is extremely vital. NO one should dwell on the "sins of the Church" and the failings of the leaders, whether Conference or independent. Because as I have always preached—when you dwell on the faults of anybody or anything, YOU WILL COME TO HATE THEM! And folks, that principle also applies to God's Church.

We are all keenly aware of the critical issues facing God's people, and there should be no excuse for us to not be rooted and grounded in our wonderful truth. But it's time for the true and faithful Seventh-day Adventists, in the self-supporting and organized work, to PRESS TOGETHER in sharing our deep burden to evangelize the world. We have a grand and glorious work to do. But Satan knows that this work can never be accomplished when God's professed people are divided, antagonistic, and unwilling to unify with each other—because one is of Apollos and one of Cephas (as we find in 1 Corinthians 1:12). And I believe the following inspired quote says it so succinctly:

"While we are not to sacrifice one principle of truth, it should be our CONSTANT AIM to reach

this state of UNITY (John 17:20)." PP 520

You may or may not know this, but since I have taken my stand to be supportive of God's organized Church, there are many voices out there who say I have "changed" and have "abandoned the truth." But folks, I still love the Three Angels' Message, the Spirit of Prophecy, and am proud to be a Seventh-day Adventist. Let me tell you from my heart that I HAVE NOT ABANDONED THE TRUTH—nor the conviction that I have to STAND FIRM for the truth! But in all honesty, I must admit that there HAS been a "change" in me. The Holy Spirit has done a wonderful work upon my heart, and revealed to me that, unbeknownst to me, in past years there have been roots of bitterness in my heart, from past situations, that needed to be removed. But now by God's grace, I no longer have these roots of bitterness in my heart towards the Conference brethren, so in that way, I guess they are right—I HAVE changed!

This working of the Holy Spirit in MY life, as well as in the lives of the other Board members of this ministry, began almost TWO YEARS AGO, with the reading of a little booklet by Ellen White entitled "The Remnant Church." Once our eyes were opened, and the scales of bitterness removed, we could discern clearly the truth—that God has an ORGANIZED Church on earth (not just a group of independent ministries doing their own thing)! And that God's one true fold is the organized Seventh-day Adventist Church, raised up by God through James and Ellen White, with world headquarters in Silver Spring, Maryland. . . .

The following Spirit of Prophecy quote makes it so abundantly clear what God's plan is, concerning MODERN DAY Israel.

> *"Mark the whole tenor of this chapter (Numbers 14), and learn the lesson it conveys to MOD-ERN ISRAEL. These things are written for ensamples to us upon whom the ends of the world are come. We see the unbelief and the stark resistance of some who have had great light, and although evidence has been piled upon evidence, they have kept themselves in stubborn resistance. The Lord has sent messages of warning and entreaty, messages of reproof and rebuke, and they, have not been in vain. But we have NEVER had a message that the Lord would DISORGANIZE THE CHURCH. We have NEVER had the prophecy concerning BABYLON applied to the Seventh-day Adventist church, or been informed that the loud cry consists in calling God 's people to come out of her; FOR THIS IS NOT GOD'S PLAN CONCERNING ISRAEL." Review & Herald, October 3, 1893*

Mrs. White has written so much inspired material on this subject, but it was this one article that was especially significant in bringing us to where we are now. It is Manuscript 21, written June 12, 1893 (you can also find this in the bound editions of The Review & Herald, Volume 6, on pages 513 to 516).

Here is the TRUE message, for God's professed people today:

> *"HOW DARE mortal man pass HIS JUDGMENT upon them, and call THE CHURCH a harlot, BABYLON, a den of thieves, a cage of every unclean and hateful bird, the habitation of devils, making the nations drunk with the wine of her fornication, confederating with the kings and great men of the earth, waxing rich through the abundance of her delicacies, and PROCLAIMING that her sins have reached unto heaven and God hath remembered her iniquities? Is THIS the message we have to bear to SEVENTH-DAY ADVENTISTS? I tell you NO! God has given NO MAN ANY SUCH MESSAGE. Let these men HUMBLE THEIR HEARTS BEFORE GOD, and in true contrition REPENT that they have EVEN FOR A TIME stood by the side of THE ACCUSER OF THE BRETHREN who accused them before God day and night." Manuscript 21, June 12, 1893*

And folks, if you're wondering why I'm writing this letter, that is ALL I am now endeavoring to do—repent, and ask forgiveness, that for a time, I stood by the side of the "accuser of the brethren," and called God's Church "Babylon."

Wow! This is so painful, but sometime ago, I came to the stark realization, that not only was my soul's salvation at stake, but thousands of other well-meaning Adventists—and I could not allow my pride to get in the way, and be the means of myself and others losing out on eternity. I would be an unfaithful shepherd if I were to continue going down a wrong road, after the Holy Spirit has revealed it to me. Going on with that same inspired quote:

> "Let every soul now seek to answer the prayer of Christ. Let every soul echo that prayer in mind, in petitions, in exhortations, that they all may be one even as Christ is one with the Father and work to this end. IN THE PLACE OF TURNING THE WEAPONS OF WARFARE WITHIN OUR OWN RANKS, LET THEM BE TURNED AGAINST THE ENEMIES OF GOD AND OF THE TRUTH. Echo the prayer of Christ with your whole heart: 'Holy Father keep through thine own name those whom thou hast given me, that they may be one, as we are. ... I pray not that thou shouldest take them out of the world but that thou shouldest keep them from the evil.' Also this prayer which He offers to interpret the process through which His followers are sanctified: 'Sanctify them through thy truth.'...
>
> "The Lord has had a church from that day, through all the changing scenes of time to the present period, 1893. The Bible sets before us a model church. They are to be in UNITY with each other; and with God. When believers are UNITED to Christ, the living vine, the result is that they are ONE WITH CHRIST FULL OF SYMPATHY and TENDERNESS and LOVE. When anyone is DRAWING APART FROM THE ORGANIZED BODY of God's commandment-keeping people; when he begins to WEIGH THE CHURCH in his HUMAN SCALES, and begins to PRO-NOUNCE JUDGMENT against them, then you may KNOW that God is NOT LEADING HIM. He is on the WRONG TRACK. . . ." Manuscript 21, June 12, 1893.

But folks, as if all this counsel was not plain enough, it was the last paragraph in this article that finally brought me under the deepest conviction!

> " We are as a church to be wide awake, and to WORK FOR THE ERRING AMONG US, as laborers together with God. We are furnished with spiritual weapons, mighty to the pulling down of the fortress of the enemy. WE ARE NOT TO HURL THE THUNDERBOLTS AGAINST THE CHURCH OF CHRIST MILITANT; for Satan is doing all he possibly can in this line, and YOU WHO CLAIM TO BE THE REMNANT OF THE PEOPLE OF GOD HAD BETTER NOT BE FOUND HELPING HIM, DENOUNCING, ACCUSING, and CONDEMNING. Seek to RESTORE, not to tear down, discourage, and destroy. " Manuscript 21, 1893 (6RH 513-516)

So, for these reasons, the Board of Prophecy Countdown has chosen to stop identifying this ministry, and ourselves, as "HISTORIC Seventh-day Adventists." We are simply SEVENTH-DAY ADVENTISTS who want to be a BLESSING and SUPPORT to God's ORGANIZED, REMNANT, WORLD CHURCH!

Some Adventists want to have nothing to do with me now, because I once believed and taught that God's organized Church had become Babylon. Then of course there's the other group (my former supporters) who believe I need to now be CONDEMNED, because I have reversed my position on that, and I am now endeavoring to abide by the counsel of the Spirit of Prophecy—that we be UNITED with God's commandment-keeping people in both the ORGANIZED and self-supporting work. But folks, I just want to be faithful to the leading of God's Holy Spirit, even if it goes against my pride and "popular opinion." Rather than condemning, it is our prayer at Prophecy Countdown that more of God's people will be rejoicing for us, and hold up our hands as we now endeavor to do a work of RECONCILIATION and RESTORATION for all those who have abandoned God's organized world Church. . . .

Thanks for allowing me to share what's on my heart!

Your brother in soul-winning,

John Osborne Founder/Speaker